D0626098

VEG
STREET

SOUTH DUBLIN COUNTY LIBRARIES	
SD900000103293	
Bertrams	12/03/2013
	£16.99
	TA

VEG STREET

GROW YOUR OWN COMMUNITY

NAOMI SCHILLINGER

SHORT BOOKS

CONTENTS

INTRODUCTION

I was brought up in South London where the neighbours were always in and out of each other's houses, borrowing cups of sugar and lending cars for big trips. Both my parents were keen gardeners, and I used to help out in the veg patch when I was young, even planting up my own strawberries. My dad often sent us out with bowls of homegrown tomatoes to share with neighbours when we had a glut.

It wasn't until about 20 years ago, when I moved into a flat with a balcony, that I became overwhelmed by the desire to grow fruit and vegetables again. The space wasn't huge, but once the growing bug returned, tomatoes ripened in pots, edible window boxes followed, filled with lettuces, and the balcony also came alive with herbs for cooking, and flowers to brighten each day.

In 2000, it felt joyous, luxurious even, to be moving to a house with both back and front gardens. It took me some years to come to grips with a shady 15ft x 45ft back garden, but a sunnier 10 ft x 10ft front garden was immediately put into use. I dug up the neat lawn to make space for my ever-increasing list of planting ideas. At this point I grew mostly flowers, with the odd herb around the edges. Somehow I didn't equate front gardens with vegetables.

Inspiration and change arrived in the unlikely guise of scaffolding when we were having our house painted. Anxious for the well-being of my plants, I moved them all from the front to the back garden. Once the painters had left, I saw the front garden as an exciting blank canvas and I decided to turn this space into a mini allotment. The soil was still fairly heavy clay, so to give seeds and plants a fighting chance, I transformed two builders' palettes into two perfectly sized raised bed frames (see how to on page 36). I filled them with topsoil and compost and was ready to get planting again. As soon as my leeks, lettuces and runner beans started coming up, neighbours started to stop and chat, eager to find out more about what was growing.

To extend my horticultural activities, I decided to build myself a min-greenhouse and was very pleased to spot some rather tasty-looking sash windows (ideal for this purpose), leaning against a wall in a front garden around the corner. Ringing the bell brought Nicolette to the door, who was very happy that her windows would be recycled. Over coffee, Nicolette told me that Islington Council were giving away free packets of wildflower seeds for tree pits (the area around the bases of street trees). We started spreading the word and sharing more of these free seeds. Before long our neighbourhood came alive with gorgeous flowers.

Since then, Nicolette and I, along with other enthusiastic neighbours, have set up our community veg growing scheme (and embarked upon a few other horticultural adventures too). First, encouraged by the initial transformation of our two streets with wild flower tree pits, we entered "Islington in Bloom" and came away with five awards, as well as a bit of money to spend on plants for our neighbourhood. Then at an Islington Gardeners meeting I heard about a veg-growing experiment that needed more growers to get involved. And ping, an idea popped up in my head: why not get entire streets involved in growing not just flowers, but veg? Between

Nicolette's local email newsletter, leafleting the area and plenty of knocking on doors, in our first year, we signed up 50 households to take part in growing vegetables in their front gardens.

For this growing experiment, runner beans, sweet corn and squash were available to grow in large growbags which we had delivered to neighbours' doors. But how to deliver the seeds? We were concerned about leaving them on top of growbags at the mercy of the weather. At this point our next door neighbour Lindsey and I came up with the idea of holding a 'Cake Sunday'. A group of us got together to bake cakes and we set up shop in a neighbour's front garden. We weren't sure how many people would turn up, but our first event was a huge success; neighbours happily staying for hours to chat, getting to know each other, and discussing growing plans.

And so our project was born.

In 2012 we celebrated our fourth growing season and we now have over a hundred neighbours growing veg in front gardens and window boxes. It's no exaggeration to say that our project has transformed the feel of the neighbourhood. Manuel, who used to farm in Spain, lives with his wife opposite us and, as a keen gardener, grows lemons, plums, beans and chillies. Julia, Seb and their four kids now have a large amount of pots and growbags in their front garden, successfully growing rhubarb, spinach, strawberries and potatoes. It's great to see their ever-expanding food production and the children taking pride in what they grow. Our neighbours Kate and Paul asked other residents if they'd like to cultivate their large corner front garden rather than see the land unused – so now we have a community plot, growing courgettes, raspberries, lettuces and beans, blackberries and asparagus and a mini wildflower meadow!

This book won't give you a complete A-Z of every fruit and vegetable out there (for that I'd recommend Joy Larkcom's 'Grow your own Vegetables' and 'Fruit' by Mark Diacono), but it's packed full of simple 'how to's' and shared knowledge gleaned from friends, neighbours and my own growing experiments over the last 20 years. It's designed to lead you through the gardening year, so that whatever month you dip into, there'll always be masses to do, whether it is ordering seeds, building a mini-greenhouse from plastic bottles, or harvesting the crops that you've grown. Nothing beats the sheer delight of growing your own or of leaning out of your window to collect food for your dinner. I do hope you will feel encouraged to have a go. Good luck!

Top left: Rushida with Cocarde lettuces. Top right: Esther with Pink Fir Apple potatoes. Bottom left: Nevil planting sugar snap peas. Bottom right: Joy Larkcom, author of the superb 'Grow your own vegetables'. Previous page: Naomi picking Terenzo trailing tomatoes

THINGS YOU NEED TO KNOW

POTS, PLANTERS, SOIL & COMPOST

Growing on window sills & balconies in pots & containers

Setting up your pots, containers and growbags can require a feat of organisation, but efforts made now will reward you all year long with fresh salad leaves, vegetables and fruit for your meals. There's nothing better than being able to pick your dinner minutes before it's eaten.

Size of window boxes & pots

If you're planting in window boxes, measure how wide your window ledges are and then buy the biggest, widest, deepest window box you can find (or make) to fit your space. The same goes for pots and containers. The bigger the better as they won't dry out so quickly and there will be more room for your plants to put down roots. Also, the bigger the container, the less watering and feeding you will have to do. Bear in mind how much weight your window sill can take and make sure the window boxes are well secured so that they can't fall.

Compost in pots

Getting the compost or soil right in your pots is key to growing successful and healthy vegetables. Lettuces, rocket and mustard leaves are quick growers and not too demanding, so will be happy growing in any multi-

purpose compost. Other fruit and vegetables such as tomatoes, runner beans, courgettes, strawberries and raspberries like it much richer, so plant them in John Innes no.3, a soil-based compost packed full of nutrients, or in your own home-made compost if you're lucky enough to have the space for a compost bin (see below). Our community veg-growing project has also successfully used the free recycled green waste compost supplied by our local council to grow vegetables in, so I'd say experiment with different types of compost; try combinations, and see which works best for you. All composts have a finite amount of nutrients, so after six weeks or so, some feeding will be necessary. You can add in 'Blood fish and bone' or 'Growmore', both general slow-release feeds, when planting into multi-purpose compost and regularly feed all pots and containers with liquid seaweed feed during late spring and summer to keep nutrients topped up.

Home-made compost

My favourite compost is my own home-made version in which the magic of worms turning kitchen and garden waste into beautiful crumbly compost never ceases to amaze me (and which I never have enough of!). With only the start-up cost of buying (or building) a bin, this is a free way of recycling green and food waste which produces a compost that has tons of nutrients and a perfect texture for vegetable growing. The only time I don't use it is when I'm sowing seeds as my compost is not weed-free and I don't want other plants competing with my tiny seedlings.

I've also stopped putting tomatoes into the compost as their seeds are so good at germinating that some years when I've grown plants in my own compost, I've had small forests of tomato plants smothering recently planted fruit and veg.

If you have enough space, wooden slatted compost bins are great (try www.primrose.co.uk for a good selection of sizes) as they allow plenty of aeration to your mix and this speeds up the process a little. However, any dustbin or large container, metal or plastic, with holes drilled in the bottom will do very well, with the advantage that they can be squeezed into small spaces. Stand the bin on a couple of bricks or pieces of wood and also drill holes around the top of the bin to encourage good air circulation.

Once you've bought or constructed your bin, add kitchen and garden waste which will take about three months to rot down over summer (in a 3-foot (1m) cube-shaped bin) and a bit longer over winter. Don't add meat or fish to the bin outside, as this can attract rats and foxes; but equally, don't completely fill with grass clippings as this will rot down into a sludgy and odorous mess. Try and add a good mix of vegetable peelings, banana skins, egg-shells, coffee grounds alongside collected leaves, dead plant material that isn't too woody (even thin tree branches will take years to rot down) and lawn clippings. You can also add old bits of cardboard and newspaper if the mix is looking slimy. In an ideal world, three compost bins would be best: one bin taking your current waste, another one with compost rotting down and the last full of compost ready to use.

If you've got no room for a compost bin, then wormeries are a great small and speedy option for rotting down all your kitchen waste into nutrient-rich compost. They're readily available online (try www.wigglywigglers.co.uk) or have a look at www.verticalveg.org.uk for a video on how to make your own wormery. It's not complicated and will save you a few quid.

Soil

Good soil (or compost) is the most important factor for growing healthy fruit and veg. It's really important to understand what your soil is like, to help your plants grow to their best potential.

Soil types Loam is the ideal mixture of clay, silt and sand, where your soil is soft and crumbly, holding onto water and nutrients, but also allowing water to drain. Most of us gardeners don't have the luxury of perfect soil, but there's plenty you can do to get your soil into good working order.

Where my parents live in South London, there are street names like Lavender Road and Lavender Vale as the soil is chalky and sandy, ideally suited for fields of lavender to grow. However, while chalky and sandy soils are light soils, easy for roots to grow in (great for carrots and parsnips), the soil is fairly poor in nutrients, and other vegetables, such as beans and peas, will need richer soil to perform well. To improve the soil, add plenty of organic matter such as compost or very well-rotted manure.

The soil where I live in North London is clay. Heavy clay soil can be difficult for roots to penetrate as the small particles that make up clay bodies are packed tightly together, but there are tons of good nutrients waiting to be tapped. Clay soil is also prone to holding onto too much water in winter and becoming too dry in summer. Again, you can improve your soil greatly by adding copious amounts of organic matter, such as compost or well-rotted manure.

Alternatively, if your clay soil is completely solid and too heavy to dig, as is often the way, you can build a raised bed on top of the clay soil – see page 36 – then fill it with compost which will allow your fruit and veg to flourish.

How can I tell what type of soil I have? Dig up some of your garden soil and rub it between your fingers and thumb.
• Loam will form crumbs in your fingers.
• Clay soil will be sticky and you'll be able to roll it into a ball or sausage shape easily.
• Sandy soil will be rough and gritty and you won't be able to get it to hold any shape at all.
• Silty soil will have a silky feel to it, and although not as sticky as clay, you'll still be able to roll it into a sausage shape.

Talk to neighbours who like gardening. They're be able to tell you straight away what the soil is like and which vegetables they find easy to grow.

How to add organic matter to the soil and the 'no dig' system of gardening January is a good time to add organic matter such as compost or well-rotted manure to your soil. If you add a 2-3-inch (5-7.5cm) layer of organic matter, also known as a mulch, to the top of the soil, worms will over time work this in for you. Some gardeners believe that digging compost into the soil instantly improves it, loosening it up and adding nutrients, whereas others are opposed to digging as they believe it ruins the structure. I find sometimes it's just not possible to dig in compost to the whole bed if it's already planted up with bulbs and other plants, so adding compost on top of the soil is the best and only option. I avoid digging my soil, especially in winter, as it kills my back, and I can also see that treading on and digging heavy wet clay soil does further compact this already dense growing medium. Whether you dig or don't dig, winter is the best time to add compost to your soil, as the cold weather will help to break down the compost structure and worms will burrow through it and aerate the soil too.

Planting into the soil

Mixed planting In a small growing space it's a great idea to have mixed beds, so that fruit, vegetables and flowers grow together. This is better for biodiversity and you can create some really exciting planting combinations, mixing rhubarb with dahlias, raspberries with scabious and leeks with Californian poppies. It'll look amazing, the flowers will attract pollinators for your fruit and vegetable plants and you'll be able to eat most of what you agree too.

Crop rotation Whether you're mixing your plantings or having small vegetable beds, it's important not to grow the same annual vegetable crops in the same space year after year. If you do, you'll get a build-up of soil-borne pests and diseases that will damage your crops. Vegetables belong to different families, and advice has traditionally been to try and avoid planting from the same family of crops into the same area within three years. Here are some of the vegetables in the different families:

LEGUMES Runner & French beans, sweet peas, sugar snap peas

BRASSICAS Cabbages, cauliflowers, Brussel sprouts, broccoli

ROOTS Potatoes, carrots, parsnips

ALLIUMS Onions, garlic

In reality, when you're growing in a small space, this three-year system isn't possible and you probably won't be growing vegetables from all the different families. Just try and move plantings around as much as possible each year. Vegetables in the legume family, such as beans and peas, will add nitrogen to the soil and help other crops grow the following year.

Space

Think about where you can grow your veg. How many hours of sun does your growing space get each day? How many pots can you squeeze in on the ground or on window ledges; in other words, how much actual soil is there to grow in?

Light

Most vegetables prefer sunlight, so the sky's the limit if you have a sunny growing space. If you have a shadier spot, perhaps go for plants such as lettuces and Swiss chard that prefer not to be in the sun all day. It's important, though, to recognise that no fruit or vegetables will grow in complete shade, so be realistic about what plants you can grow in your available light.

Fruit and veg that will grow in a shadier spot, but with at least 3 hours of sun a day:

VEGETABLES	FRUIT	HERBS	FLOWERS
Lettuces	Rhubarb	Mint	Violas
Rocket	Wild strawberries	Parsley	
Japanese & mustard leaves	Raspberries	Coriander	
Swiss chard	Japanese wineberries	Chives	
Jerusalem artichokes	Blackberries	Sorrel	
Spinach, tree spinach	Blueberries	Chervil	
Kale		Sweet Cicely	
		Salad burnet	

Other fruit and veg that need at least 5-6 hours of sun a day:

VEGETABLES	FRUIT	HERBS	FLOWERS
French & runner beans	Strawberries	Marjoram	Sweet peas
Tomatoes		Oregano	Nasturtiums
Leeks		Borage	Cornflowers
Carrots		Lovage	Wildflower mixes
Peas, pea shoots		Sage	Nigella
Mangetout, sugar snap peas		Rosemary	Hollyhocks
Beetroot		Lavender	Sunflowers
Squash & courgettes		Tarragon	Daylillies
Potatoes		Basil	Tulips
Garlic			Daffodils
Kohlrabi			

Right: 'Red Solix' oakleaf lettuces, with spiky green Mazur lettuces, purple violas and orange marigolds

THIS MONTH'S LIST

JANUARY

While it's cold and bleak outside, you can snuggle up in the warmth and settle down to some serious planning for the year ahead. There's always a different vegetable or variety to try out and as the new year begins the gardening possibilities that lie ahead are incredibly exciting. Many vegetables are annuals – ie harvested the same year in which you planted the seed – which gives you an almost blank canvas in January to decide what you'd like to grow. Successes can be built upon, and experiments that didn't work can be learnt from. If you're growing fruit and vegetables for the first time, begin by imagining what you'd like to eat later in the year and then grow what you love. With space (and time) always at a premium and after a number of years of experimenting, I now plump for fruit and veg that I find truly delicious and flowers that fill my heart with joy.

🏠 COMMUNITY CORNER 🛒

Nicolette and I initially started up our neighbourhood growing scheme to brighten up our streets by growing flowers around the bases of our tree pits. Little did we know that five years on, we'd be involving over 100 households in our area in growing vegetables in their front gardens and expanding our activities even to the creation of a magnificent herd of topiary elephants on one of our street corners (see page 186).

What originally inspired us was that our local council (Islington, London) was giving away free packets of wildflower seeds. We gathered enough packets of seeds to share with 20 or so neighbours, enabling them to sow their seeds in tree pits alongside their houses. We then met up with these neighbours over tea and coffee and hatched some exciting gardening plans. Our enthusiasm for greening up the area galvanised everyone into action and we found that there was a real appetite for getting to know one another.

The free seeds from our local council (for that year) helped us get started, but if you're strapped for cash, try approaching your local gardening organisations through the Royal Horticultural Society (http://www.rhs.org.uk) for help, or contact a few seed companies to see if they offer discounts or free giveaways. It's also worthwhile contacting your local council to see if it funds any community projects, although you may need to form a constituted group to receive funds. This sounds much more complicated than it is – you'll need just three or four neighbours and a little bit of time to get started (see page 205). If you want to involve more neighbours, start knocking on doors. Many people will be happy to join in and contribute, whether by giving their time, or simply providing useful materials – spare plants, pots and window boxes. Start building up a list of neighbours who are enthusiastic about participating. Most people use email these days, but where we live, there are lots of neighbours who aren't online – particularly older folk – so knocking on doors is a really important aspect of how we stay in contact with everyone and make sure neighbours are included (if they want to be!).

Top left: Annual poppies grown in a tree pit
Top right: Manuel protecting his lemon tree in his front garden
Bottom left: Manuel clearing a neighbour's path
Bottom right: Neighbours at a Cake Sunday

SOWING & PLANTING
VEGETABLES

Planning what to grow

This is such an exciting and enjoyable task and one that I look forward to every winter. Inevitably I overdo the ordering, and come the spring, I have the difficult task of finding enough space for my fledgling nursery.

First of all, decide which vegetables, fruit and edible flowers (see page 25) you would like to grow and make a list. Next, draw a rough plan of your growing space, be it a number of pots and containers or some flower/veg beds in your front garden.

Most fruits are perennials, occupying their space year after year, so if you're plumping for fruits, plan where these will be planted and the leftover space will dictate how much room will be available to grow your vegetables in. Having said that, you can often fit in two crops in the same container or space during the year. Early potatoes will be dug up by mid-June or July and their pot can be used again for vegetables including kohlrabi, radishes, carrots, mangetout, kale or beetroot. Likewise, early 'Paris Market' carrots grown in a window box (yes, you can! See page 52) can be followed by some quick-growing cut-and-come-again lettuces. Dwarf sugar snap peas sown in an old suitcase in April and harvested in July can be followed by sowing Swiss chard, mustard leaves or spinach in August for overwintering.

Also, think about which crops can maximise your yields. French and runner beans perform brilliantly growing up tall canes or washing lines, and training courgettes and mini squash to climb supports is another great use of vertical space.

Ordering vegetable seeds

Below I've listed some of my favourite seed companies which, between them, supply a great selection of quality seeds. This is where dinner from your doorstep begins!

www.chilternseeds.co.uk – many heirloom varieties (and an entertaining read).

www.sarahraven.com – fabulous images and honed vegetable selections.

www.nickys-nursery.co.uk – great seeds with high germination rates according to *Which?* gardening trials.

www.seaspringseeds.co.uk – a wide array of chilli seeds and plug plants and other veg too.

www.organiccatalogue.com – a dazzling array of organic seeds.

www.higgledygarden.com – fantastic flower seeds with many informative and entertaining 'how to's'

www.pomonafruits.co.uk – great strawberries and fruit bushes.

There's also Franchi-seeds of Italy, Thomas Etty and all the big boys, including Marshalls, Thompson and Morgan, Suttons, Mr. Fothergill's (and more!)

Left: 'Paris Market' baby carrots

Ordering seed potatoes

Seed potatoes (they look just like small potatoes) are now widely available to buy online from specialists and all the major seed companies. It's amazing how many varieties of potatoes there are available to grow and they come in all shapes, sizes and colours. Seed potatoes ordered in January are usually posted out in February, ready for planting in March. Also, as the 'grow your own' movement is undergoing a revival, 'Potato Days' are becoming increasingly popular all over the country. These events, normally held in January, February and March, offer a vast array of modern and heritage seed potato varieties. You can buy potato tubers individually, allowing you to try out a number of different varieties. If you have room for only one growbag for potatoes, you'll just need to buy three tubers. Check with the Potato Council www.potato.org.uk or www.potatoday. org/potatodays.htm to see where your nearest event is happening this year.

Potatoes are normally listed according to when you can harvest them: **First earlies** are quick growers, ready for digging up about 10-12 weeks after planting. If you plant in mid-March, they'll be ready to eat by early June. **Second earlies** take a little longer, about 15 weeks. **Main crop and late varieties** take 20-22 weeks before you can harvest them and are ready in July, August and September.

If you have limited space, then I'd plump for growing first earlies as most maincrop potatoes are readily available in the shops. As my gardening friend Veronica once said, 'Digging up potatoes is like hunting for treasure.' There's nothing like excavating your own spuds in early summer, and after years of growing potatoes, I'm still delighted every year by what I've managed to grow. I've found 'Foremost' to be a tasty and reliable cropper. 'Sharpe's Express' is also a delicious first early potato, but with lower yields. 'Charlottes' are a good second early, cropping well and with a waxy texture that makes them ideal for boiling whole or for salads.

The only 'late' potato I grow is 'Pink Fir Apple', which you can harvest at the beginning of September. Loved by chefs and diners alike, these knobbly nutty tubers are a real treat at the end of the summer and, along with my first earlies, are a crop that I religiously grow every year. If you do have a bit more space, I would recommend any of the gorgeous heritage potatoes (main crop). On the other hand, if you like a bit of a novelty, then you could opt for 'Salad Blue' earlies, which will give you lilac mashed potatoes for dinner. There's also the stunning purple-skinned 'Arran Victory' (see September harvesting) or the red-skinned 'Highland Burgundy Red', with mostly red insides, for more quirky culinary creations. (All available from Carroll's Heritage Potatoes www. heritage-potatoes.co.uk).

Chitting potatoes

What exactly does 'chitting' mean? Well, chitting just means encouraging potatoes to sprout before they are put into the ground, especially useful in getting early varieties off to a flying start. Once your tubers have arrived, place potatoes with the end with most 'eyes' upwards in egg boxes or trays. Make sure they are placed in a frost-free, cool, light position such as an unheated spare room or a garage or shed with windows. If there is not enough light, the shoots will become pale and elongated, which will weaken the potato and be more likely to snap off during planting.

Chitting isn't essential, however, and if you've bought your potatoes at the end of March, you can also plant them straight away (see page 55).

Top: Buckets of potatoes at Potato Day
Bottom: Chitted potatoes ready to plant

SOWING & PLANTING
FLOWERS

Planning for edible flowers

Lots of flowers are both edible and great for attracting pollinators. You may already have flowers in your garden or on your window sill that you didn't realise were edible. Many gardeners grow chives for their tasty leaves, but the flowers also add a gorgeous oniony flavour to salads. Both wild and cultivated rocket produce flowers at the end of their growing cycle throughout the summer and both have a mild but sweet peppery flavour. My favourite edible flower is the nasturtium. Nasturtiums can be yellow, orange or deep, deep red and have a lovely, crunchy, hot peppery taste. They're relatively big, so they always make an impact in the salad bowl. Borage is also delicious, with its subtle cucumber taste. Flowers such as hollyhocks, cornflowers, daylilies and violas don't have strong flavours, but will certainly add different textures and a whole heap of colour to your salad bowl.

Stuffed courgette flowers are a rare delicate summer treat; try them filled with ricotta cheese and a mix of herbs, coated with a light batter and quickly fried, and you'll decide courgettes are worth growing for the flowers alone!

Hollyhocks, daylilies and chives are perennial plants, coming back year after year, and can be bought in pots to plant out in your front garden. Rocket, borage, cornflowers, courgettes and nasturtiums, on the other hand, are annuals that can easily be grown from seed, so add any of these to your seed ordering list.

Planning for pollinators

No bees, no veg! Bees fertilise all your crops by transferring pollen and seeds from one plant to another, so it is important to plant plenty of flowers that are good pollinators. (Some popular flowers look wonderful, but have been overbred and bees can't get to the nectar.) Perennial herbs such as marjoram, oregano, chives, lavender, bergamot (used to flavour Earl Grey tea), echinacea (the cone flower) and the lesser-known but gorgeous hyssop (Agastache) will certainly do the trick, coming back year after year, providing great flavours for the kitchen and beautiful flowers for the garden. These plants can easily be grown from cuttings or bought as small plants from garden centres.

And annuals will also play their part. Sowing seeds is a cheap and easy way to invite bees into your plot, and there are plenty of candidates that will attract them, such as sunflowers, the poached egg plant, Californian poppies, love-in-a-mist, cosmos and pot marigolds. You can also buy the most gorgeous annual meadow mixes, full of colour. We plant these around the bases of our street trees every year in April (see page 77). When looking for good plants for pollinators, I found the online Chiltern Seed catalogue really useful – it highlights nearly 400 bee-attracting plants. Sarah Raven (www.sarahraven.com) has a beautifully illustrated A-Z list of pollinator friendly plants and the RHS (Royal Horticultural Society) also lists a whole number of bee-friendly plants for your garden at www. rhs.org.uk

SIMPLE BUT BRILLIANT IDEAS

||||||||||||||||||||||||||||||||||||||||||||||||||||||||||||||||||||||||||||||||

Outfoxing the foxes

These suitcases are wonderful containers for sowing seeds, but have proven to be equally popular with the local wildlife as the perfect toilet spot. To discourage this behaviour, break up a few bamboo canes and stick them in the soil at different angles so that the animals can't easily access the bare earth. Better still, if you have some old rose clippings with spiky thorns, these make a great barrier for deterring both foxes and cats. The sticks can be removed when the plants are big enough to fend for themselves, but should protect them from visiting wildlife when they are small and easily damaged.

ONE POT SHOP

START COLLECTING CONTAINERS

Spend time this month hunting for containers for the year ahead, so that, as things get busier in spring, you'll be ready to get planting. Try and get the biggest containers possible to fit your space as the more soil available, the better the plants will grow. Having said that, it's also fun to experiment with quirkier containers, planting herbs and lettuces in teapots, colanders and tin cans, but just be aware that these smaller containers are high maintenance and demand watering daily or even twice a day in scorching weather. You'll have to feed them more regularly too.

Old wooden wine boxes from wine merchants are great planters, being nice and deep, and will fit perfectly onto wider window sills. They'll rot after a few years, but line them with heavy-duty plastic, such as old compost bags, and they'll last for a good bit longer. Old galvanised bowls and tubs are great, but they're certainly quite rare to find these days without a rather large price tag attached! Terracotta pots may be heavier for lifting onto window ledges, but they look gorgeous and roots will remain cool and happy in clay.

Plastic containers may not always be as stylish as terracotta or metal, but they retain water, they're light, easy to move around and come in a multitude of shapes and sizes. In fact, any container with holes drilled into the base can be planted up to produce a fantastic edible display.

Top left: Swiss chard. Top right: African basil will attract bees for months over summer. Bottom left: Chives. Bottom right: Nasturtiums

THIS MONTH'S LIST

FEBRUARY

By now I'm itching to place my seed order(s) and desperate to start sowing. Sadly, light levels and temperatures are still too low to begin sowing most seeds outdoors. Mind you, there are tons of jobs to be getting on with to prepare for the growing year ahead. And, if you are really keen, you can start sowing indoor seeds with the help of a heated propagator. Although not essential for most seeds, heating the pots from the base will speed up the germination process and although it may seem like an extravagance, you'll use a heated propagator throughout the spring and year after year if your passion for vegetable growing increases.

For anyone who has only a small amount of outdoor space, a mini greenhouse is one of the best investments you could ever make. These tall, thin structures with shelves for seed trays are covered in clear plastic sheeting to protect seedlings from the cold and wind (£15 at www.wilkinsonplus.com or make your own version by recycling plastic bottles – see December, page 194). The transparent covering allows enough light for early sowings to grow without becoming leggy, and lettuces and mustard leaves can be started off from mid-February to produce leaves that will be ready to crop in April (mustard leaves) and May (lettuces).

You could try sowing a few mustard leaf and radish seeds outside in pots, but this is a hit-and-miss exercise, depending on the weather.

🏠 COMMUNITY CORNER 🛒

Having sown our free seeds from Islington council, our flourishing flowering streets drew much admiration and this encouraged both Nicolette and me to enter our streets in the 'Islington in Bloom' competition. We won five prizes and some very useful money in the first year, and this also led to a fortuitous invitation to a meeting of the Islington Gardeners (a local gardening association). By lucky chance, one of their members was looking for more volunteers for an experimental growing project. He already had funding and we only had to conjure up some willing participants to receive free growbags and seeds. This is when we started knocking on doors in earnest in our North London streets; and we signed up 50 willing participants in just a few months.

From then on things have gone from strength to strength. Having good relations with the council has enabled us to access a whole range of free services to assist with our scheme – whether it be free compost, or help from a Community Payback Team (offenders on community service) who spend a day loading 100 large growbags for us.

February is the month in which we liaise with the council about most of these things – to contact the compost recycling centre and book in a compost delivery, order the growbags and coordinate with the Community Payback organisers. At the same time, we place our seed orders and get together with our core of neighbours to decide on a date of the delivery for the growbags and also for our next community get-together when we will give away the seeds.

We've found that different neighbours bring different strengths to our project. Bernd has become an expert in securing funding for removing concrete from front gardens. Ten front gardens have been transformed from ugly concrete to cherished green spaces already. Nicolette produces a local email newsletter which goes out to over 500 households in the area, and manages to find free containers and plants that we can share with neighbours. Recently I was chatting to Liesbet, who really loves sunflowers, and she said she'd like to organise growing 300 sunflower seeds (with a little help from the rest of us!) to give away as plants in May. A simple idea, easy to execute, and one that will have a huge impact once those generous yellow blooms are in flower. It really is great to work together to green up an area. As my neighbour Judith says, 'This project has brought a real feeling of belonging – the best of village life to the centre of London – a feel for the seasons changing, and hope for the next year to come.'

Top left: Nicolette with runner beans
Top right: Blue cornflowers and daisies in a tree pit
Bottom left: Sunflowers in a front garden
Bottom right: Bernd in his front garden

SOWING & PLANTING

VEGETABLES

Sowing lettuces & Swiss chard in a mini greenhouse

Sowing lettuce seeds and other leaves such as Swiss chard in a mini greenhouse will give you a head start on your veg sowing. There are several wonderful varieties of lettuce to choose from (see page 51 for my favourites). Swiss chard comes in a lovely mixture called 'Bright Lights' which, with its colourful red, yellow, pink, orange and white stems, never fails to please

You can use any container for sowing seeds as long as it's a couple of inches deep and there are holes in the bottom for drainage. I often use empty plastic supermarket food containers. I also find that sowing in modules can be a useful way to start off your veg. Modules give each seed an individual space, so that roots aren't disturbed when planting out or potting on into a larger container.

So onwards with the seed sowing: I use New Horizon multi-purpose compost to sow my seeds in, just sieving the compost for the top inch or so in a pot to make it a little finer. This allows the young roots easy access to water and nutrients.

Almost fill your container with compost, using about an inch (2.5cm) of your sieved compost at the top. Water your compost before sowing seeds.

If I'm using modules, I usually sow two seeds per module and thin the seedlings out later to leave the strongest one happily growing away. If planting seeds in trays, sow thinly (see page 202).

Always read the packet as to how deep you need to sow your seeds. Lettuce seeds are very fine, so will need just a light covering of compost after sowing. Swiss chard seeds are bigger, so sow them about half an inch (1.3cm) deep. Water in with a fine hose or watering can so that the seeds are not displaced by a heavy rush of water.

TIP

If you haven't got a watering can with a fine rose, this would be another worthwhile investment. You'll use it again and again when planting seeds and it makes the job of watering your seeds much easier, and more successful in the long run.

SEEDS TO SOW THIS MONTH
Mini greenhouse: Lettuces, swiss chard, rocket, mustard leaves
Indoors: Sweet peas

Top: Sieving compost to give fine soil for sowing seeds into
Bottom: Seedlings growing in modules

Making raised beds

If you have problem soil, or no soil at all, then a raised bed could be the answer if you're desperate to get out there and sow vegetables.

After my 10ft x 10ft front garden was cleared of plants to make way for the painters, I decided to convert it into a mini allotment. Neighbours had some old palettes lying in their garden, waiting to be taken to the recycling centre, and I used these to build two raised beds on top of my rather unpromising heavy clay soil. Here's how:

YOU WILL NEED *a sledge-hammer, crowbar, saw, regular hammer and nails.*

STEP 1. Use the crowbar to deconstruct the palette. First remove as many nails from the outside of the slat as possible.

STEP 2. Then, get the crowbar right under the slat, hammer it in and gently prize the slat away from the post, being careful not to be too gung-ho and split the slat in the process.

STEP 3. Hammer out any remaining nails. Et voilà! You will have wood, ready to build your raised bed.

STEP 4. Saw the posts in half, so that you have eight smaller posts.

STEP 5. Then start nailing slats to each post.
For the centre posts, the slats should be nailed to meet in the middle of the post.
For the end posts, nail the slats right to the end of each post. I made my raised bed two slats high as I had plenty of soil to fill it with, but you could always make it one slat high too.

STEP 6. Nail the end slats on, position your raised beds and dig in the posts. Fill the beds with a good mixture of topsoil and rich compost. I put bark chippings in between the beds, so I don't get too muddy picking veg and flowers. It took me an afternoon to break up the palettes and construct and fill two raised beds.

TIP Any found object, such as an old suitcase, can be used as a mini raised bed.

STEP 1.

STEP 3.

STEP 5.

STEP 6.

🪴 SOWING & PLANTING 🍓

FRUIT

Cutting back autumn-fruiting raspberries & replanting the canes

Although it can seem quite bleak out there, small signs of life are appearing in your garden and it's time to cut back autumn-fruiting raspberries before new shoots appear. If you haven't planted raspberries yet and would like some, there's still time to order and plant some canes (see pages 185 and 200) If you have summer-fruiting raspberries, don't cut canes back now, as they produce fruit on the stems that grew last year, and if you cut these now, you'll have no fruit this summer!

If you can already see a few tiny green leaves at the base of the plant, be very careful where you prune, so as not to disturb these new shoots. These will become the canes that produce fruit in the summer

Raspberries, if kept in check and well fed, can stay in the same bed for many years; even in a large growbag, they can manage for a few years before needing to be potted on into another container with fresh soil.

Cut back all the canes with a pair of secateurs, so that only 2-3 inches of the canes are left and then give your raspberries a good mulch.(see page 204).

If your raspberries are creeping away from where they were originally planted, dig these extra canes up and cut the roots off with secateurs as they'll still be attached to the original plant. These extra canes can be planted elsewhere or given to a neighbour.

Top: Cutting back autumn-fruiting raspberries
Bottom: Green shoots on autumn-fruiting raspberries

🌱 SOWING & PLANTING 🪣

FLOWERS

Sowing sweet pea seeds indoors

Some hardy seeds can be sown straight into pots or growbags outdoors from around mid-March onwards as the hours of daylight lengthen and temperatures rise. Sweet peas are one of these more hardy seeds, but they can also be sown indoors now, stealing a bit of time so that they flower in June. It's a great idea to sow some indoors now and some outside in March, so you'll have sweet peas flowering in your front garden all summer long.

The choice of sweet peas is vast, with new cultivars being launched every year.

My favourite varieties are 'Flora Norton' a delicate pale blue, 'Matucana', a two-tone delight of light and deep pink, and 'Albutt Blue',

a white flower artfully tinged with pinky purple. All are highly scented.

Sadly, I'm not an owner of a swanky greenhouse (I'm jealous of anyone who is!); however, here's where my heated propagator comes into its own.

No room or money for a heated propagator? Not a problem. A plastic bag with an elastic band to retain the moisture will do equally well and seedlings will just take a little longer to appear.

Always read the packet as to how deep you need to sow your seeds. Most need to be planted 2-3 times their depth, but some varieties such as 'Cleome' actually need daylight to germinate.

SO HERE'S HOW:

I usually sow two or three seeds into a 3-inch (7.5cm) pot.

STEP 1. Almost fill the pot with your compost leaving half an inch (1.3cm) at the top unfilled.

STEP 2. Make holes about an inch (2.5cm) deep with a pencil and drop one seed in each hole.

STEP 3. Cover the holes with a little more compost and water the pots really well.

STEP 4. If you are using a heated propagator, put the pots in and turn the heat on. Check the pots every day and make sure that the compost doesn't dry out. A week later and all the seeds will be germinating beautifully. A sight to fill your heart with joy! Germination will take

longer if you're using the plastic bag system. And remember – different veg and flowers seeds can vary as to how long they take to germinate, so do be patient as it could easily be at least a couple of weeks and sometimes longer before you see any signs of life.

STEP 5. Once the seeds have germinated, move the seedlings outdoors into a mini greenhouse if you have one, so they have more light and less heat and don't become too leggy. Then harden them off (see page 204) before planting out in April. If you don't have a mini greenhouse, move your seedlings to a bright but cooler spot inside so that they develop sturdy stems. Don't pack away your heated propagator yet. There'll be plenty more use for it in March and April!

SIMPLE BUT BRILLIANT IDEAS

||||||||||||||||||||||||||||||||||||||||||||||||||||||||||||||||||||||||||||||||||||

Volunteering

A simple but brilliant way to improve your gardening knowledge is to volunteer. There's nothing like working alongside an expert and getting hands-on experience to increase your horticultural skills, and gardeners tend to be very willing to share their know-how with others.

'Food from the Sky' is an amazing rooftop garden, above Thornton's Budgens supermarket in Crouch End, North London. Food is grown all year round and sold to the supermarket below, using zero food miles. And it encourages volunteers to get involved.

I've also volunteered a number of times at the wonderful gardens at Great Dixter in East Sussex, alongside Fergus Garrett and his knowledgeable and friendly team. It's a heavenly environment to work in and I've picked up numerous propagating and gardening skills as well as massively increasing my plant knowledge.

Some gardens set aside specific days for volunteers, but if you know of a particular garden where you'd like to offer your time, it's always worth asking. They are likely to be delighted to have extra hands.

ONE POT SHOP

MUSTARD LEAVES IN A MINI GREENHOUSE

You will need:

1. A container to fit in your mini greenhouse (plus bubble wrap to line it if your container is made of metal)

2. A crock for drainage

3. A soil sieve

4. Multi-purpose compost – I use New Horizon, but any compost will be fine

5. A selection (or just one variety if you prefer) of mustard leaf seeds (see tip opposite)

STEP 1. Whatever container you use, make sure there are holes in the bottom and drill some if necessary. If you're using a metal container, line it with bubble wrap.

STEP 2. Place plenty of crock (broken bits of old pots and crockery) at the bottom of your container for good drainage.

STEP 3. Nearly fill your container, leaving 2 inches (5cm) empty at the top. Sieve enough compost to add another inch of compost to the top.

STEP 4. Label where you are going to sow, and make half-inch grooves in the soil with your finger or a pencil, as this is the depth at which mustard leaf seeds need to be sown. Water soil well.

STEP 5. Thinly sow seeds in grooves (see page 202) and cover with sieved compost.

STEP 6. Water in well with a fine hose or watering can.

STEP 7. Place whole container in your mini greenhouse. Keep well watered, not letting the soil dry out.

STEP 8. After 7-14 days, tiny shoots will appear. As seedlings develop, thin them out (see page 202) so that plants are about 3 inches (7.5cm) apart. Thinnings can be eaten in salads as micro greens. Harden them off (see page 204), bringing your container outside in about a month. Keep picking outer leaves as plants grow, leaving the inner leaves to carry on developing.

STEP 1

STEP 2

STEP 4

STEP 7

STEP 8

TIP

Experiment with as many different varieties as you can to find the mustard leaf that you like best. Here, I have sown 'Red Frills', 'Green in snow', 'Red Knight Mizuna' and 'Golden Streak', alternating reds and greens and frilly and solid leaves for contrasting colours and textures. They've all got quite different tastes, some stronger than others.

THIS MONTH'S LIST

MARCH

March is the busiest month of the year. My excitement rises in tandem with the temperature, as seeds can be sown outside and finally, after what seems an eternity, the clocks go forward. Hurrah!

People seem to be out more tending their own front gardens, everyone enjoying the first days of spring. Daffodil bulbs that we gave away last autumn are glowing a glorious rich yellow, and there's the promise of later varieties such as 'Pheasant's eye', flowering later in April.

Be guided by nature as to the timings of sowing seeds outside, as you'll begin to notice self-seeded plants popping up when the temperatures reach just the right level outside for germination. There's still just time to order and plant bare-rooted fruit canes and bushes such as raspberries and Japanese wineberries (see page 185) and now is the best time to order strawberry plants, with different varieties supplying delicious fruits from April until October. (see page 52).

COMMUNITY CORNER

Once our project was off the ground, my next-door neighbour Lindsey and I were scratching our heads as to the best way to distribute seeds to all the participating neighbours. We came up with the idea of holding a get-together in a front garden, in keeping with our veg-growing plans. Cake seemed like a fine idea to lure neighbours along, and in April 2009 we launched our first 'Cake Sunday' with more leaflets and knocking on doors. The first Cake Sunday exceeded all our expectations, with neighbours not only turning up to collect seeds, but staying for an hour or two, happily getting to know one another. These gatherings are an excellent way of increasing the feeling of neighbourliness. As Julia, whose children are keen growers, put it: 'The project has been great for our community spirit. I feel safer and feel that my children are safer. It can get a bit like *The Archers* at the Cake Sundays – though I haven't quite

worked out which one is Linda Snell yet! Very nice to have a bit of the country in the heart of London.' We now hold Cake Sundays two or three times a year. In spring we give away vegetable seeds, and in autumn we give away bulbs to enliven our streets in the following year. In the last few years, we've also delivered large 2-foot (60cm)-square growbags to everyone's front gardens, full of free compost from recycled green waste. (Thank you Islington Council!). The delivery day is quite a feat of organisation, making sure everyone gets a growbag for the year ahead. The bags themselves are fairly heavy but we've now developed a good system, hiring a van with a tail lift and trolleys to pull the bags along. And it's all well worth it in the end, when you see a cornucopia of vegetables growing in front gardens later on in summer.

Top: Neighbours, Robert and Helen, chatting with a Community Police Officer at a Cake Sunday
Bottom: Choosing bulbs at a Cake Sunday

SOWING & PLANTING

VEGETABLES

Lettuces & other leaves – which varieties to choose?

We eat salads all year round, and I love being able to go out in the front garden and pick my dinner five minutes before we eat. But when it comes to salad leaves, don't just stop at lettuces. Tree spinach (*Chenopodium giganteum*) has very decorative, unbelievably bright pink leaves; nasturtium leaves have a lovely refreshing succulent taste, as do pea shoots (see June's One PotShop, page 108); and mustard leaves always add a zing to a salad, as well as gorgeous textures. And don't forget herbs. Chervil will add a gentle aniseed flavour and sorrel a lemony bite. All can be sown now.

There are so many lettuces out there to choose from that it can be bewildering, but here are few varieties that I enjoy growing. I love a Cos lettuce and have found 'Freckles' to be fantastic for taste and longevity; I find I can crop it for a good three months. I also love mixing colours and textures in the bowl, so a red oakleaf such as 'Solix' or the more pointy 'Cocarde' are favourites too (all available from

sarahraven.com). If you like a soft sweet leaf try the bright green butterhead 'Arctic King' (available from Chiltern Seeds), which is good for overwintering as the name suggests. This year I'm also experimenting with Mazur, a spiky frisee head, as part of *Which? Gardening* trials. It looks great and adds another texture to the salad bowl. So have a hunt around and try out a few different varieties each year to find the lettuce you love to eat.

Lettuces do very well in less sunny parts of the garden, so save your brighter growing areas for more sun-loving vegetables. Lettuce seedlings sown inside in February can be hardened off (see page 204) this month, then planted out in April, ready to eat in May. Lettuces sown now will be ready to eat a little bit later; sow in small batches from now on, every four to six weeks and you'll have home-grown salads all summer long.

I sow my seeds mostly in modules (see page 35) so that I have small seedlings which I can plant straight out either into pots or into the ground when the time is right or space becomes available.

SEEDS TO SOW THIS MONTH
Outdoors: Lettuces, mustard leaves, spinach, kale, coriander, Swiss chard, kohlrabi, chervil, lovage, sorrel
Mini greenhouse: Carrots, leeks, tree spinach, beetroot

Lettuces (left) 'Arctic King',
'Solix' and Cos 'Freckles'

Growing carrots

You wouldn't think that window boxes were deep enough to grow carrots, but there are some varieties, such as 'Paris Market' (available from www.chilternseeds.co.uk) that are gorgeously small and almost spherical (about the same size as a golf ball) and ideally suited for growth in a shallow-ish container. Here's how:

Almost fill a window box or any container with John Innes no.2 compost (A soil-based compost that doesn't dry out quickly).

Scatter seeds thinly (see page 202) when sowing and cover with a fine layer of compost. Water in with a fine rose so as not to disturb your seeds with a big gush of water.

When seedlings are just large enough to handle, thin to about 2-3 inches (5-7cm) apart to give the seedlings enough space to develop into decent-sized carrots.

If you want to grow larger carrots, then use a bucket or similarly deep container which is at least a foot (30cm) deep. Carrots will grow very well in a large container.

If you're planting into the ground, carrots like fine, deep, fertile soils and will really struggle in heavy clay soils. They'll also fork if they hit stones. (A good reason to grow carrots in pots where you have control over the soil).

To deter carrot fly (other than putting up fine netting to 2ft (60cm), try fooling them by mixing in annual flowers. Nigella has very similar foliage to carrots and looks great alongside the crops. Alternatively, grow carrots in with your flowers as they have lovely decorative foliage and if left in the ground, they will produce cow parsley-like flowers the following year too.

Carrots come in many shapes and sizes and amazing colours too – white, red, yellow and purple – so it is worth doing a little research to find out which varieties are on offer before you choose what to grow. As well as the 'Paris Market' and 'Early Nantes' varieties, why not try 'Rainbow Mix' for its rich multi-coloured roots from www.pennardplants.com or the tempting 'Cosmic Purple' variety from www.nickys-nursery.co.uk

---

Ordering strawberry plants

Now is the time to order three types of strawberry plants that will give you sweet delicious fruits from April until October. (See how to plant on page 137).

Cultivated varieties are strawberries that we usually buy in the shops and fruit in June and July. With cultivated varieties, go for taste, not for size. 'Cambridge Favourite' has a fab flavour and needs to be planted in full sun for best results.

Wild strawberries are much smaller in size than their larger relations, and they crop from April until July. Their berries are intensely sweet and a little tart at the same time, hitting your taste buds like no other fruit can. Their low growing habit makes them ideal for edging pathways and planting in window boxes, and they can even take a little shade.

And then there's the fantastic 'Mara des Bois' perpetual strawberry (see harvesting on page 160) which will give you tasty juicy berries from July until October. As 'Mara des Bois' has some wild strawberry parentage, this fruit will grow in a little shade too. Plants can be ordered from: www.pomonafruits.co.uk and www.kenmuir.co.uk

Top right: Small round 'Paris Market'
carrots grown in a window box
Bottom right: Early 'Nantes' carrots
grown in a bucket'

Planting potatoes

Potatoes bought in January and February should be chitted (see page 22) by now and ready to plant. Mind you, whether chitting is beneficial or not is a matter of hot debate in the veg world. And all potatoes, chitted or not, can be planted from about mid-March. Remember, though, that they are susceptible to frosts, so never plant into hard and frozen ground or if temperatures are below freezing, as this will kill your lovely tubers. Wait until April to get going.

Planting potatoes in containers and growbags I've used all sorts of containers to grow potatoes in very successfully. You can buy 40-litre growbags from seed suppliers such as Marshalls, but any large pot, old dustbin or even heavy-duty bin liner is ideal.

1) Half fill your growbag or container with John Innes no.3 compost, garden compost or council recycled green waste compost.

2) Position three or four tubers evenly on the compost, chitted end or 'eyes' pointing upwards. The bigger the container, the more tubers will fit.

3) Cover the tubers with compost, until the container is about about three-quarters full.

4) Water in well and keep well watered throughout the growing season.

5) When the leaves reach about 8 inches (20cm) high, start earthing up (see page 69).

6) After about four weeks, feed with liquid seaweed every week to get the best crops.

Traditionally, potatoes are grown in the soil by digging trenches or holes to plant the tubers in. However, I've also had great results by growing the potatoes straight on top of grass, with harvests of 5lb (2.27kg) per tuber. It may seem strange, but the roots should be able to grow down through the grass and, in my garden, the tubers do not appear to be hampered by my heavy clay soil at all. So if you have a spare two or 3ft (60-100cm) of grass, give it a go. You will be delighted and amazed by the results.

Planting potatoes on top of grass Try this method from 'no dig' guru Charles Dowding.

1) You can weaken the grass by covering with cardboard for two or three months, but I plant on top of fresh grass and this works well for me.

2) Make small mounds of compost 12 inches (30cm) apart

3) Nestle a seed potato into each mound, chitted end or 'eyes' pointing upwards.

4) Carefully cover with 6 inches (15cm) compost.

5) Earth up (see page 69) when leaves are about 8 inches (20cm) tall.

Planting potatoes in the ground

1) If the soil is a bit tired and old, dig in a good few inches of compost to improve it as this will really improve your potato yield.

2) You can either dig a trench 6 inches (15cm) deep and plant tubers 12 inches (30cm) apart or just dig individual 6-inch (15cm) holes, 12 inches (30cm) apart.

4) Plant tubers into the holes or trench with their chitted ends or 'eyes' pointing upwards.

5) Fill trench or holes with soil or compost.

4) When leaves are about 8 inches (20cm) tall, start to earth up (see page 69).

Top: Positioning potatoes in bin
Bottom: Potatoes nestling on top of grass

Choosing tomato varieties & sowing tomato seeds

Tomatoes definitely need a warm and sunny (minimum six hours of sun a day) site to perform at their best and ripen. There's a vast array of tomato varieties to choose from. Some need to be grown in a greenhouse to have any chance of ripening, but there are plenty more that will ripen well outside in a warm English summer. (Although a cold wet summer will have many a tomato grower reaching for a green tomato relish recipe!)

Last summer I went to the Victoriana Nursery in Kent for a tomato-tasting session. There were over 30 varieties on offer and I picked a few different ones to try out this year as well as my favourites, which I know work well in my garden. That's the point. Experiment and see what grows best for you. Tomatoes can be a tricky veg to grow, but through trial and error (and I've made plenty of mistakes!), you'll find the ones you can grow successfully and which, most importantly, you like the taste of. Nothing can beat the taste (and intoxicating smell) of a warm tomato freshly picked from the plant.

My favourite to date is 'Sungold', which is a small orange cherry tomato. Achingly sweet, perfect for salads and a plant that I know does well in a large pot on our patio. Lizzie, who I garden with regularly, rates this tomato highly too. This year I'm experimenting with 'Outdoor Girl', a very small salad tomato (a bit bigger than a large cherry tomato) and 'Black Krim', a monster of a tomato with rich and meaty flesh. I'm also trialling 'Terenzo', a tumbler variety (available from Thompson and Morgan) that seems very robust and that, as I write, is producing an abundant crop of tasty bright red cherry tomatoes in my window boxes.

Colin, who's moved house a number of times over the last few years, has perfected the art of growing his entire garden in pots and found that 'Yellow Tumbling Tom' was a huge success, providing oodles of sweet cherry tomatoes throughout July and August.

Another neighbour, Lucy, recommends 'Money Maker' for a reliable haul of cherry tomatoes in pots and is also trying out 'Shirley's Pixie', a salad variety for the first time. Neighbour and ace tomato grower David recommends 'Gardeners Delight', an old reliable cherry tomato, and grows his plants as cordons directly in the soil in his south-facing back garden.

The difference between cordon and bush growing What's a cordon? I hear you ask. Growing tomatoes as *cordons* means encouraging the central stem to grow, tied into a tall cane, to about 8 feet high–they really do grow that tall!–and pinching out most of the side shoots (except the ones forming flowers for fruiting). This tall thin method of growing allows you to grow a lot of tomatoes in a small space. Many tomatoes can be grown as cordons, but there are some, such as 'Sweet pea currant' and the tumbler 'Terenzo', which are best grown as a *bush* to give you the maximum yield of tomatoes.

Bush varieties throw out lots of side shoots to form a bushy framework. You'll need to use a few canes with string ties to contain the tomatoes as they grow, otherwise they tend to flop onto the ground. By the way, 'Sweet Pea currant' are tiny tomatoes, great for tiny fingers and as the name suggests, very very sweet. 'Terenzo' are great for window boxes or hanging over the edge of a large container and are hefty producers.

Whichever method you use, you should always completely remove the lowest leaves to reduce the risk of the plants developing tomato blight.

How to grow tomatoes Tomato seeds can be sown indoors in a 4-inch (10cm) pot from about mid-March in multi-purpose compost, about eight weeks before you plant outdoors in May (see page 91). Once they start putting on growth, they'll quickly take up a fair amount of room, so make sure you can accommodate these prima donnas in a warm and sunny site indoors for the next couple of months! If you don't have space, not to worry. All the major seed companies offer small tomato plants to buy which they'll send out to you in May and small plants are always available at local garden centres and markets.

Growing beetroot

My favourite beetroot has to be 'Chioggia' for its immense decorative quality when sliced open, as well as its sweet taste. Young beetroot leaves can be added to salads and older leaves cooked as you would spinach leaves, which makes this a great-value veg. Like carrots, beetroots come in many shapes and colours. You could try 'Burpees Golden' for its beautiful yellow colouring, 'Pablo' for smaller tear-shaped roots, or 'Cylindra' for 8-inch (20cm) long cylindrical roots (you'll need a very deep pot to grow this).

I tend to start an early sowing of beetroot in my mini greenhouse in March, planting in modules, so that seedlings can be planted out in April and May into pots or the garden.

You can start directly sowing outdoors in April and all the way through until July. Beetroot will take about three months to grow, depending on how big you want the roots to be, so plant every four to six weeks and you'll have beetroot from summer and well into autumn.

NB. If you are growing it in a container, beetroot needs a depth of at least 12 inches (30cm) to accommodate its long roots.

Sow seeds very thinly (see page 202), about 2-3 inches (5-7.5cm) apart and later thin these out to about 4 inches (10cm) apart for their final growing position. Beetroot seeds are unusual as they are multi-celled seeds. This means that you'll get two or three plants growing from each seed that you sow. Some people leave these plants to battle it out, but I have more success when I thin them out to one plant per sowing position. The more space you allow these roots, the bigger they will grow, so I like to pick beetroots when they're somewhere between the size of a golf ball and a tennis ball to get the sweetest of flavours.

Choosing rhubarb crowns

If you're passionate about rhubarb and want to be able to harvest these tasty stems from spring all the way through until September, then it's worth checking out different rhubarb growers and seed companies for varieties that crop at different times of the year. Brandy Carr Nurseries is a specialist grower in Yorkshire and always offers a pack of three varieties, often 'Timperley Early', cropping in April and May, followed by other varieties that could supply you with rhubarb right up until the end of summer. My mum insists that 'Champagne' is the sweetest variety. I also love the look of plants with deep red stems such as 'Raspberry Red' and 'Canada Red'.

Rhubarb will grow in some shade, but does need at least three or four hours of sun a day to grow well. Plant in a bed which has had plenty of well-rotted manure added a few weeks before planting if possible, or in pots with equally rich soil or John Innes no.3 compost. Rhubarb can grow well and look magnificent in pots, but make sure it's a big pot (at least 12 inches or 30cms in diameter and depth) for the plant to reach its full stature.

Here's the tricky bit. Don't eat any stems in the first year. The plant needs time to establish itself before you go pulling off stems. Plants will last for years if given this first season to develop well, so tempting as it is, hold back until year two of growth.

Left: 'Chioggia' beetroot

SIMPLE BUT BRILLIANT IDEAS

||||||||||||||||||||||||||||||||||||||||||||||||||||||||||||||||||||||||||

Plant labels

It's wise to label your pots and rows so that you know where you've sown your crops. Don't forget to write the date alongside the variety of veg, as this can give you valuable information on how long your seeds have taken to germinate – always good to know for next year.

Plastic labels are widely available from garden centres, but you can create your own labels too. I've found that the classy wooden cutlery that comes with some takeaways makes a great recycled plant label.

ONE POT SHOP

HOW (AND WHY) TO RE-POT MINT

You will need:

1. Your old pot of mint

2. Fresh compost-John Innes no.2 for your pot and multi-purpose compost for small cuttings in pots

3. Extra 3-4 inch (7.5-10cm) small plastic pots for extra cuttings

4. A pair of secateurs

Mint is such a versatile herb for cooking, making mint sauce, mint tea or gracing a glass of Pimms in the summer. It can grow in full sun or a shadier spot as long as it gets three or four hours of sun a day. It's best not to grow mint in the ground, as it will run amok, crowding out most plants in its wake, taking over whole areas in a garden. However, as mint is such a fast mover, it outgrows its pot very easily and can quickly become pot-bound and die. I re-pot my mint every year and this gives me the opportunity to pot up cuttings for friends and family too.

March is a good time to start re-potting; in spring growth is vigorous. But you can re-pot mint throughout the summer, and up until early October if it's still mild-ish, that should be fine but remember new growth will be much slower in early autumn.

STEP 1. Turn your pot upside down and remove your mint. You'll be able to see that all the new roots are jammed against the outside of the pot. All these roots can be used for re-potting – although I like to use the younger roots as this rejuvenates the plant.

STEP 2. Refill your mint pot with fresh soil.

STEP 3. Cut about four or five lengths or pieces of root and re-pot to the same depth that they were in before. Place the cuttings in the middle of the pot, which will give them space to move outwards again. Water the container and in a matter of weeks your mint will be growing better than ever.

STEP 4. Water in all cuttings and keep them well watered.

STEP 1.

STEP 3.

THIS MONTH'S LIST

APRIL

The days are becoming delightfully longer and warmer. It's great to have extra time and light as there's so much to do. Seeds sown in late February and March will now need to be potted on outside, and there's a whole army of other seeds waiting to be sown. This is the month when all your plans hatched during the long winter months become a reality as fledgling leaves pop up through the soil. Every time I see a fresh green shoot, I'm amazed by the miracle of growth. I've bought a couple of mini greenhouses to line the side of our house, but there's never enough room for all the vegetables I'd like to grow. So veg ideas that can't be fitted in now join the list for next year's attempts. My kitchen also starts to become a temporary greenhouse with potted-on tomatoes filling up much of the available window space and other less hardy seeds, such as courgettes and cucumbers, germinating in pots draped with plastic bags or clingfilm. Having friends round for dinner can be a tight squeeze, as they negotiate the maze of pots strategically placed near all available light, to reach their seats at the table.

COMMUNITY CORNER

In our neighbourhood, the whiff of spring encourages everyone into action. People take real pride in the tree pits, weeding and then planting them up again with the annual wildflower seeds that we give away each year. Over the last four years, we've grown either French or runner beans as part of our community veg-growing project. These edible climbers are great for planting in a large container or growbag as they make very good use of relatively small spaces with their vertical growth. If watered well throughout the growing season, you'll eat like kings from a single pack of seeds and children will be fascinated to watch their own giant beanstalks reaching for the clouds.

Our green growbags have been a huge success and alongside beans, neighbours are now growing potatoes, courgettes, leeks, tomatoes, Jerusalem artichokes and some very decorative rhubarb plants.

We have also dipped our toes into other horticultural activities, planting up forgotten areas and working with neighbours to bring unloved front gardens back into use.

One year, with the resident's permission, we planted 300 tulips in his otherwise empty front garden, which come the following spring wowed the garden owner and passers-by alike.

Tulips are like gems in spring. They're so vivid and they usually last for a good few weeks. My favourite is the orange 'Ballerina' tulip seen here paired with the gorgeously frilly, deep pink 'Curly Sue'. If you have room for one pot, then have a go at growing these beauties, as they'll give you colour at a time when most other plants are only beginning to pop their heads up above the soil. (Make a note to order bulbs later in the year for next spring – see page 153). I've found that tulips won't return with the same glorious vigour again if grown in pots or heavy clay soil, so I remove the bulbs when they've finished flowering and compost them. An extravagance, I know, but well worth it for the colour and joy they bring when they give of their best. Pots can then be reused for planting up edibles for later in the year.

Other bulbs that we've grown in the neighbourhood, such as daffodils, will have finished flowering by now. Don't be tempted to cut back their foliage, though, as these stems will be photosynthesising like crazy to store up as much food as possible to help the bulbs flower next year. Give them a helping hand by feeding with liquid seaweed every week or so, until the foliage has completely died back.

Right: Orange 'Ballerina' tulips were planted alongside deep pink 'Curly Sue' to give a vibrant and uplifting front garden display

How & why you earth up potatoes

Once they've started growing, your potatoes will need to be 'earthed up' to protect your precious crop from going green if they come into contact with daylight – and this should increase your yield too. Three or four weeks after planting your potatoes, robust meaty leaves will start appearing. When the leaves are 6-8 inches (15-20cm) tall in a container, carefully cover most of the foliage up, leaving just an inch or so sticking out. In a short time, you'll be delighted to see the leaves growing again, stronger than ever. This may seem counter-intuitive, but you won't harm the plant or make the leaves rot by doing this and hopefully you'll also get more potatoes. If your potatoes are in the soil or growing on top of grass, scoop up the surrounding soil or add extra soil or compost to create a mound around the foliage, again leaving just a little bit popping out at the top. You can repeat 'earthing up' once or twice more as the potatoes continue to put on more growth, but stop when the plant starts to flower.

SEEDS TO SOW THIS MONTH

Outdoors: Lettuces, carrots, beetroot, chard, kale, spinach, sweet peas, seed potatoes, peas and pea shoots, annual flowers, wildflower mixes, lovage, sorrel, coriander, parsley, nasturtiums, hollyhocks
Indoors: Tomatoes, French and runner beans, courgettes, squashes, pumpkins, basil

Left: Henry earthing up potatoes grown on grass

Sowing courgettes, squash & runner & French beans indoors

In mid-April, I start sowing seeds for these less hardy vegetables indoors so that they'll be ready to plant outside in May when there's no chance of frost. They take about five to six weeks to develop a good enough root system before they can be planted out.

I usually sow these larger seeds either individually in 3-inch pots or with two seeds in a 4-inch pot, sowing them about an inch and a half (3cm) deep. This way, I don't disturb the roots when planting out in May. Once planted, cover the pots with a plastic bag or place in a propagator (see page 41). Seedlings should start to appear 7-14 days later. If space is an issue, you can hold off sowing seeds until May when you can plant all seeds directly into pots, containers and soil outside. This just means you'll have your crops a little later.

Runner bean 'St. George' is a vigorous grower with lovely red and white flowers and tasty beans; while the purple French bean 'Cosse Violette' is a stunning addition to any front garden with its heart-shaped leaves and beautiful pink flowers.

'Tromboncino' courgettes produce a wonderful trombone-shaped vegetable – beautifully decorative and easy to grow vertically up canes in tight, but sunny spaces.

> **TIP**
> I've found that French beans hate being too wet and will rot before they germinate if soil is too damp – so only water once when sowing and then wait until leaves appear before watering again. Squash and courgettes seeds can rot too, so plant the flat seeds vertically. In this way, you'll avoid water gathering on their flat surfaces in the soil.

Successional sowing

Now that the soil has warmed up, sow little and often. This will give you a succession of crops throughout the summer. For example, sow a small row or container of beetroot, carrots, peas and lettuces now and repeat the process in three or four week's time. Continue sowing little and often over the next few months. I've found planting in modules (see page 35) is a great way of starting off vegetables, as once they are big enough to plant out, you can fill in gaps and plant up containers with seedlings that have a headstart.

Left: Runner beans emerging

Sweet peas, mangetout & peas

Sweet peas sown indoors in February (see page 41) should be big enough to be hardened off (see page 204) and planted outside. Don't panic if you haven't started growing sweet pea seeds yet. You can start them off now. It means that you'll have flowers a month or so later. Or you can buy them ready grown from garden centres or from online seed companies. They'll germinate more quickly if sown indoors, but they are hardy plants, so can also be planted directly outside. Just watch out for slugs.

For most of the pea family, including sweet peas, peas and mangetout, a teepee makes a great vertical climbing frame, but I struggle every year to find enough pea sticks in my urban environment to make this work. A pea stick is any twiggy stick, the bushier the better, up to 5 feet (150cm) in length that will provide support. (Once these plants start growing, they produce thin wiry tendrils that need more support than a simple bamboo cane can provide.) If not available locally, pea sticks can be ordered online (try Hazel Woodland Products). But actually pea netting (available from all large DIY shops and garden centres) or string, artfully wrapped around bamboo canes, will do just as well.

First, using three or four 8-foot (240cm) bamboo canes or long sticks, make a basic teepee shape and tie canes together at the top of the structure. Then add in your pea sticks, netting or string, filling out the teepee shape. Try not to leave gaps, as the tendrils will need continual support as they wind their way up the structure. When you are satisfied, plant your sweet peas all around the base of the teepee and water well. I normally plant around 10-15 pots of sweet peas, depending on how wide the teepee is at its base. Seeds sown in February should be flowering in June and July, and those sown now should flower in July and August.

Herbs

Try out some more perennial herbs that you'll be hard-pressed to buy in either local greengrocers or supermarkets. Lovage has an intense celery flavour and is great for soups, a herby pesto and for flavouring chicken; sweet cicely has a gentle aniseed taste and is a natural sweetener for rhubarb; sorrel has a crunchy lemony taste and is great for both salads and soups; salad burnet has a subtle cucumber flavour for another interesting salad leaf and tarragon is an elegant plant, also with a gentle aniseed flavour. Lovage and sweet cicely are large clump formers, so will eventually take up 2-3 feet (60-90cm) in a bed, but salad burnet, tarragon and buckler-leaf sorrel would happily sit in the front to middle of a border or grow in a medium-sized pot.

Marjoram, sage and rosemary can also be tricky to get hold of in the shops but will happily grow in window boxes and pots look great when edging a path up to the front door. Their flowers are also loved by bees. All herbs are available from www.herbalhaven.com·

Top left: Sweet cicely. Top right: Buckler leaf sorrel
Bottom left: Salad burnet. Bottom right: Lovage

How to plant out leek seedlings

Whether you've grown leeks from seed or bought them as tiny plants, now is the time to start planting them out. Don't worry if you haven't started sowing yet as there's still plenty of time. Try and stagger your sowing in order to have a succession of crops throughout autumn and winter and baby leeks during the summer as well. Leeks will grow into big chunky plants if they have the space, so allow 9 inches (22cm) between plants and a foot (30cm) between rows if sowing into the soil. However, if you want to taste the delights of baby leeks you can plant them a lot closer together: 3-4 inches (7.5-10cm) for tender leeks in August and September. Small leeks grow well in pots too. Whether you are putting them into soil or into pots, the seedlings are ready to go outside when they are about 6-8 inches (15-20cm) tall.

STEP 1. If you've bought leeks and they look a little pot-bound (ie roots all squashed together and tangled up), give them a very good soak to loosen the roots before planting out.

STEP 2. With a stick or pencil, make a generous hole for your leek.

STEP 3. Let the leek drop into the hole and then water it in. There's no need to firm the leek in with your hands as the water has helped the roots make contact with the soil. Water the soil if it doesn't rain and make sure that soil in pots never dries out.

Leeks are a really useful winter vegetable that you can continue to harvest from October until February or March, when other pickings in the garden can be slim.

STEP 1

STEP 2

STEP 3

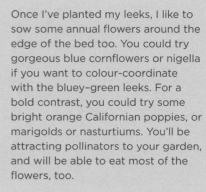

TIP

Once I've planted my leeks, I like to sow some annual flowers around the edge of the bed too. You could try gorgeous blue cornflowers or nigella if you want to colour-coordinate with the bluey-green leeks. For a bold contrast, you could try some bright orange Californian poppies, or marigolds or nasturtiums. You'll be attracting pollinators to your garden, and will be able to eat most of the flowers, too.

❦ SOWING & PLANTING 🪣

FLOWERS

How to sow annual flower seeds

Sown now, annuals will miraculously appear just a couple of months after planting, to give you a burst of fresh flowers in late spring and summer. They're great for filling gaps in your beds, planting in pots or creating mini meadows around the bases of trees. They will also attract all-important pollinators into your garden.

1. First you need to prepare the soil in which the seeds can flourish. Weed the whole area thoroughly, and dig to a depth of 3-4 inches (7.5-10cm).

2. You're aiming to have fine crumbs of soil to plant into, so rake it over, removing any large stones and breaking up any large lumps.

3. If you're planting a large area, mark it out into metre squares with string or bamboo canes so that you can see where you have already sown and where is left to cover. You can mix the seed with fine sand to help you see where you have been, but this isn't at all essential.

4. Scatter the seeds evenly, carefully reading (and following) sowing rates of seed per square metre on your packet.

5. Gently rake over the soil again, but don't completely bury the seeds, as some may need light to germinate.

6. Sit back, wait and let nature do its thing. You shouldn't need to water the seeds in as it will eventually rain, and they will be fine until then.

Wildflower mixes

Wildflowers will attract all manner of insects as well as providing flowering displays that will delight you and your neighbours. Sow annual mixes now and plants (depending on the weather) will be flowering at the end of May or the beginning of June.

Wildflowers are readily available as both annual and perennial mixes and can be sown as per the instructions above. Pictorial Meadows in Sheffield offer mixes that are designed to flower well into autumn in a range of mouth-watering colours and textures. Nicky's Seeds in Essex

offer a dizzying 48 mixes to encourage bats, bees or butterflies; their seeds suit different soils and habitats, including clay, chalk, coastal and copses. And Sarah Raven has cut flower meadow mixes in many tantalizing colour combinations. Most wildflowers should be sown in a sunny position, as they need at least six hours of sun a day, but there are also mixes specially created for shadier areas. Annual mixes should be sown roughly at 2.5-3g per square metre and perennials at approximately 1g per square metre, but always follow the sowing instructions on the seed packet.

SIMPLE BUT BRILLIANT IDEAS

||||||||||||||||||||||||||||||||||||||||||||||||||||||||||||||||||||||||||||||||||||||||||||||||||

The paddling pool watering system

I borrowed this great idea for keeping my plants well watered while I was on holiday from my neighbour, Nicolette.

Make sure the plants are well watered before placing them in the paddling pool and fill the bottom of the pool with an inch or two (3-5cm) of water to give them a good head start. Then, simply ask a neighbour to check that the paddling pool hasn't dried out completely if you're away for a long time. It's easy for them to top up levels in the pool with a watering can (or hose if there isn't a hosepipe ban). If they live right next door, they might even be able to direct their own hose over your garden wall!

Easy to fold up and store away when not in use, the paddling pool watering system is an ingeniously simple and effective idea. Thanks, Nicolette.

ONE POT SHOP

CREATING YOUR OWN EDIBLE WINDOW BOX

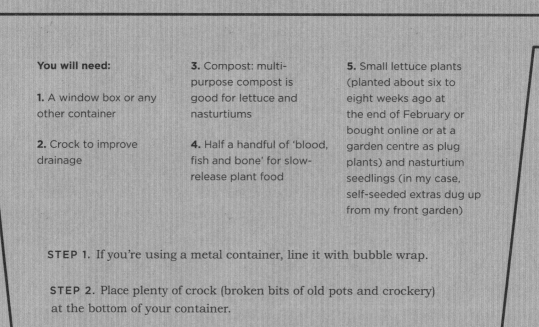

You will need:

1. A window box or any other container

2. Crock to improve drainage

3. Compost: multi-purpose compost is good for lettuce and nasturtiums

4. Half a handful of 'blood, fish and bone' for slow-release plant food

5. Small lettuce plants (planted about six to eight weeks ago at the end of February or bought online or at a garden centre as plug plants) and nasturtium seedlings (in my case, self-seeded extras dug up from my front garden)

STEP 1. If you're using a metal container, line it with bubble wrap.

STEP 2. Place plenty of crock (broken bits of old pots and crockery) at the bottom of your container.

STEP 3. Mix 'blood fish and bone' thoroughly into the compost and almost fill the windowbox, leaving roughly an inch (2.5cm) at the top.

STEP 4. Place plants roughly where you are going to plant them, keeping the nasturtiums to the side of the window box to encourage them to tumble over the edge. Make a hole in the soil for each plant and put seedlings in, topping up with compost where necessary and firming plants in with your fingers.

STEP 5. Water in plants well. Even if it's constantly raining, window boxes will dry out quicker than you'd expect, so keep them well watered. After approximately six weeks, feed every fortnight or so with a general plant food, such as a liquid seaweed feed or Growmore.

TIP

Be playful when planting out home-grown or bought lettuce seedlings, mixing colours and textures, such as a curvy red oakleaf lettuce with a more upright green Cos lettuce. My neighbour Colin often buys living lettuces from supermarkets and plants these up in pots with marigolds, providing himself with many salads from this cheap purchase and supplying colour and edible flowers to boot.

HARVESTING

In April, you're relying mostly on crops that you've sown in the previous year, such as leeks and chard (and broccoli, if you have the space to grow it) and, as these crops are eaten, April and May can be lean times. If you've not got huge amounts to pick this month, plan ahead for next year. Sow leeks and broccoli now and make a note to sow chard, perpetual spinach, mustard leaves, rocket and hardy lettuces in August and September so you won't have a hungry gap next year!

Mustard leaves

Kathryn (below) sowed mustard leaves on her balcony at the end of February. Seeds have been sown fairly thickly, allowing for plenty of peppery pickings for salads as she thins out her crop.

Opposite page: Pick the last of your perpetual spinach now before it sets seed. Below right: Flowering rocket

Radishes

These are quick growers too and seeds sown earlier in the year will spice up a salad. They also lend a colourful addition to the mix.

Flowering rocket

Rocket sown in autumn is now going to seed. Before the seeds form, try some of these delicious flowers in salads to inject a sweet and mildly peppery taste. Leave some of the flowers to develop into seeds and you'll never have to buy rocket again.

Perpetual spinach

This plant is such good value. Sown in September, it's still producing now. April is about as late as you'll be able to pick from this sowing though, as soon it will finish growing and set seed.

THIS MONTH'S LIST

MAY

This is such a fantastic time of year. As days lengthen, shoots appear just a few days after you've sown the seeds. Once the tiny leaves start forming into stronger seedlings, about three or four weeks after sowing, it's a good idea to start off another batch so you will have an uninterrupted harvest of crops throughout the summer, be it carrots, peas, lettuces or beetroot. If like me you need constant reminders to get jobs done, put a note in your diary to remind you when next to sow.

While carefully nurturing all your seedlings, it's easy to forget about perennial fruits in pots and containers, such as strawberries, raspberries, blueberries and rhubarb. All these plants will benefit from regular feeding now with liquid seaweed to encourage them to produce the tastiest of crops.

Do carry on earthing up and feeding your potatoes (see page 69). In fact, anything growing in pots will have used up the nutrients in the compost after about six weeks and, unlike plants growing in the soil, they won't be able to access any more. All this watering and feeding can be time-consuming, but the more attention you lavish on your fruit and vegetables now, the more benefits you'll reap through wonderful harvests later in the year.

🏠 COMMUNITY CORNER 🛞

May always makes me think of the Chelsea Flower Show and now also the wonderful Chelsea Fringe (www.chelseafringe.com). Independent of the flower show, but with events happening at the same time, the Chelsea Fringe is a fantastic new initiative that spearheaded over 100 gardening projects in London for the first time in May 2012. It's a celebration of all things horticultural – pop-up gardens (both indoors and out), community growing projects, art installations and cookery workshops. It was such a success that plans are afoot to spread the idea to other parts of the country.

Our participation in the first Chelsea Fringe consisted of a souped-up version of Cake Sunday, where the public were invited to join us for tea and cake and hear more about our project. Liesbet, Annie, Graham and Nicolette convened a bunting workshop and metres of colourful flags were lovingly created to hang in our street. On the day, neighbours took charge of different events: Nicola initiated many into the art of seed bomb-making (see page 94) and also organised some very entertaining vegetable races for children. Annie, a master gardener, offered quality growing advice and gave away free seeds and seedlings to all who came. Tim Bushe (our local creator of magnificent topiary sculptures) gave a virtuoso topiary demonstration and we had a cake stall brimming over with a mouth-watering selection of home-made cakes. We even had a 10-minute play in a front garden about stealing veg from a community plot. To round the afternoon off, Tim Richardson, the director of the Chelsea Fringe, presented trophies to the winners of our 'Best tree pit' competition, which had been judged earlier in the day by Veronica Peerless, deputy editor of *Which? Gardening*. The afternoon was a triumph, especially as we lucked out with the sunniest weekend for months.

Top: Naomi discussing edible window boxes with Kathryn and Alex. Bottom: Making bunting. Previous page: Uplifting allium 'Purple Sensation' – adored by bees

SOWING & PLANTING
VEGETABLES

Thinning out carrots

Even if you've sown your seeds thinly (not too close together), you will probably still have to remove some of the tiny seedlings to allow enough space for the carrots to grow into decent-sized vegetables. Small round 'Paris Market' carrots, which are ideal for window boxes and containers, still need to be thinned to about 2 inches apart.

As you thin carrots, they give off a carroty smell which, annoyingly, can attract carrot flies. The good news is that these insects cannot fly above 2 feet high, so carrots grown in window boxes or on balconies happily avoid the risk of a nasty surprise. The carrot fly will lay eggs in the root and maggots will then emerge, devastating your crop as they eat their way out. If you're growing carrots in the soil, surround your crop with fine mesh or bubble wrap up to 2 feet high (60cm) before you start thinning your seedlings. It's best to set up your protection as soon as you've planted your seeds.

Planting out & sowing runner beans

Runner and French beans are half-hardy and, like courgettes and tomatoes, shouldn't be planted out until the risk of frosts is over. Beans like good rich soil, so John Innes no.3, your own garden compost or council recycled green waste is great for a container. Or you could add well-rotted manure or garden compost to your soil to improve it before planting. When your plants have been hardened off (see page 204), position your poles in your growbag or in the soil and plant one or two plants around each pole. These beans are amazing and will cling on and climb rapidly up their supports without any help.

If you haven't started your beans yet, now is the perfect time to plant seeds straight into the soil or into a growbag outside. Be a little more generous with your sowing, planting three beans around each pole, in case of slugs or snails. I've found 'St. George' is a very reliable and tasty runner bean with lovely red and white flowers, and 'Cosse de Violette' is a gorgeous purple French bean, with beautiful pink flowers and very attractive heart-shaped leaves.

SEEDS TO SOW THIS MONTH
Outdoors: Lettuces, peas and pea shoots, French and runner beans, squash, courgettes, beetroot, kale, carrots kohlrabi, leeks, lovage, parsley, sorrel, seed potatoes, basil, tree spinach, mustard leaves, nasturtiums, sweet peas, wildflower seeds, hollyhocks, sunflowers

Top: Lindsey thinning out carrots
Bottom: Nevil with runner beans, ready to plant out

Self-supporting sugar snap peas

All peas can be sown outside from March until June. 'Sugar Ann' (available from www.seaspringseeds.co.uk) is a lovely sugar snap pea where the whole sweet crunchy pod can be eaten. It grows up to 18 inches (45cm), and is ideal for growing in a container as it doesn't need any supports, and crops about 10-12 weeks after planting.

Peas like rich soil, with compost added, so if I am sowing in a pot I use my own garden compost or John Innes no.2 compost. I think multi-purpose compost just isn't rich enough to get the best out of them.

Scatter peas as evenly as possible and not too close together, about 1-2 inches (2.5-5cm) apart, in your pot or container and cover with 1 inch (2.5cm) of compost. Water in well and keep doing so throughout the growing season, being especially vigilant if temperatures start rocketing.

You can eat the whole delicious pod as soon as you see small peas forming inside, or wait a little longer until they have filled out a bit: even then you can still eat the whole juicy pod.

Tomatoes – the next step

If you've grown tomatoes indoors (see page 57), you'll need to harden them off before planting out (see page 204). If you haven't sown your own tomatoes, small plants are still easy to get hold of in garden centres, from online seed companies and often at your local greengrocer

Tomatoes will grow well in pots, but make sure they are big enough – at least 10 inches (25cm) diameter – and equally deep, filled with John Innes no.3 compost, a good garden compost or compost from a bought tomato growbag. I find growbags on their own are too shallow for tomato roots, so I cut out the bottom of a 9-inch plastic pot, place it on top of the growbag, like a funnel, and fill it with extra compost. This way the roots will get the extra depth of soil that they need. This is really important, as if the roots dry out when the fruit is growing, blossom end rot (see page 119) which be encouraged, which could ruin your tomatoes!

STEP 1. Cut off the first set of leaves and ensure that this part of the stem is buried.

STEP 2. Water in well.

STEP 3. Put a tall 6-foot sturdy cane into the pot, and tie the stem to the cane . Keep on tying in the plant to the cane as it grows to give it support, especially as the fruits start forming. Try and water regularly at the same time each day as uneven watering can cause tomatoes to split and may also encourage blossom end rot.

STEP 4. After six weeks, start to feed with liquid seaweed or tomato feed every week.

> To avoid tomato blight, a nasty disease that could kill off your whole plant, remove any lower leaves that are touching the soil and water straight onto the roots, trying not to wet the leaves. **TIP**

Top: Henry (and Sidney) planting sugar snap peas
Bottom left: Cutting off bottom tomato leaves
Bottom right: Cutting off leaves touching the soil

Planting out climbing courgettes & squash

By mid-May it's about time to plant out your carefully nurtured and hardened-off (see page 204) seedlings. You can also buy small courgette and squash plants from garden centres around this time.

If there's any chance of frost, hold off as this could wipe out your crops. Either plant directly into the soil or into a large container – and I mean large. These vegetables are hungry and need lots of rich soil. They're often planted into the tops of large compost heaps as these are such a rich source of nutrients.

This year I've planted a 'tromboncino' courgette into an old suitcase and built a bamboo ladder for it to climb up. I feel I should start singing 'Stairway to Heaven' every time I see this picture! If you have a small but sunny gardening space, these climbers are a great way to squeeze in tons of veg.

As I say, these are greedy growers, for which a multi-purpose compost just isn't rich enough, so always use John Innes no.3 compost or your own garden compost. Once planted, water in well and keep on religiously watering and feeding all summer long. You'll be delighted with the results. You can train all sorts of courgettes and small squashes up your own specially devised supports, but larger pumpkins are too heavy for this growing system and will need to be spread out along the ground. They can be started off in large pots, though, and will happily run riot, covering up heaps of unsightly concrete, and other plants, if you let them.

Flowering rhubarb – don't panic!

Rhubarb normally flowers at the end of summer, but if it is flowering now, just cut off the flowering stem to allow your plant to produce juicy stems throughout the summer.

Adding straw to strawberries

As the fruit starts forming, pop some straw (available from pet shops) under the strawberries to stop them from rotting when they come into contact with the soil.

Right: 'Tromboncino' courgette planted in a large suitcase, with plenty of vertical support

SIMPLE BUT BRILLIANT IDEAS

||||||||||||||||||||||||||||||||||||||||||||||||||||||||||||||||||||||||||||||||||

Making a seed bomb

Seeds bombs (clay balls with seeds mixed in) are a fantastic way to green up inaccessible areas in your neighbourhood and are really easy to make. May is the perfect time to sow wildflower seeds. All you'll need is:

Some powdered clay (available from your local art shop hopefully or www.bathpotters.co.uk)
Wildflower seeds
A plastic bowl
A jug of water
An apron
A chopping board or piece of wood for rolling out clay (optional)

STEP 1. Measure out 5 parts clay powder to 1 part wildflower seeds.

STEP 2. Put the wildflower seeds and powdered clay into a plastic bowl.

STEP 3. Add enough water to make a sticky dough-like consistency – you don't want to make it too watery a mix!

STEP 4. Mix together with your fingers – it's a messy business so wear an apron or old clothes.

STEP 5. Take a small amount and roll it in your palms to make a ball. If you want to be more creative, you can form the clay into all sorts of shapes – don't make them too intricate, though, as once the clay is dry, these objects will be very fragile.

STEP 6. Let the clay balls or shapes dry out for a few days.

STEP 7. Find an unloved piece of land that would benefit from some wildflowers and throw your seed bomb into the area. As it rains, the clay will easily break down, the seeds will be dispersed and will then grow into beautiful wildflowers. Simple but brilliant!

ONE POT SHOP

GROWING A GREAT SALAD MIX IN A COLANDER

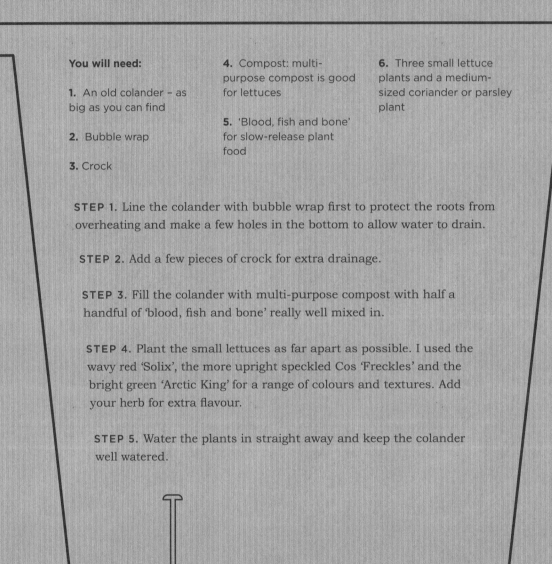

You will need:

1. An old colander – as big as you can find

2. Bubble wrap

3. Crock

4. Compost: multi-purpose compost is good for lettuces

5. 'Blood, fish and bone' for slow-release plant food

6. Three small lettuce plants and a medium-sized coriander or parsley plant

STEP 1. Line the colander with bubble wrap first to protect the roots from overheating and make a few holes in the bottom to allow water to drain.

STEP 2. Add a few pieces of crock for extra drainage.

STEP 3. Fill the colander with multi-purpose compost with half a handful of 'blood, fish and bone' really well mixed in.

STEP 4. Plant the small lettuces as far apart as possible. I used the wavy red 'Solix', the more upright speckled Cos 'Freckles' and the bright green 'Arctic King' for a range of colours and textures. Add your herb for extra flavour.

STEP 5. Water the plants in straight away and keep the colander well watered.

TIP

Afterthought! As you can see in the pic, right, the coriander has disappeared under the lettuces. The lesson here is to give the coriander its own pot in the future or choose a larger plant that will be able to compete with the lettuces!

May is one of the quietest months for harvesting as all the overwintering vegetables have been eaten and most of the new fruit and veg are still a month or so away. However, there are still some delicious pickings to be had.

If you're passionate about rhubarb and want to extend the cropping season, check out different rhubarb growers for different varieties that crop at different times of the year. Brandy Carr nurseries in Yorkshire always offer a pack of 3 varieties with one variety, often Timperley Early, cropping in April, followed by other varieties that could supply you with fruit right up until September. My mum always says 'Champagne' rhubarb is the sweetest variety on earth.

Rhubarb

The first fruit of the year. Depending on the weather and the varieties you have growing, you may have already started cropping this wonderful fruit in late March and April too. Pull stalks, grasping them right at the bottom, and always leave enough stalks and leaves on for the plant to continue to grow well. If you pick too many stalks now, the plant won't be able to photosynthesise and build up enough energy for cropping in subsequent years.

Wild strawberries

If you haven't tasted these, then rush out and buy a plant or two now (from www.wigglywigglers.co.uk). They're very different from their larger relatives – intensely sweet and they'll fruit, on and off, from April until August. They're small compact plants, but do well planted in clumps. And it's best to plant a few plants if you want to fill a bowl as the fruits are quite small! However, they spread easily over time, throwing out long thin runners which form new plants nearby.

Violas

Violas are another edible flower that will really add interest to a salad. You can grow them from seed, but these hardy plants are easy to buy, and in so many beautiful varieties, that I usually save my precious growing space for more difficult-to-grow crops. When I have lettuce or mustard leaf seedlings ready to plant into a window box or container, I add a couple of small pots of violas to the mix to create an even more decorative display.

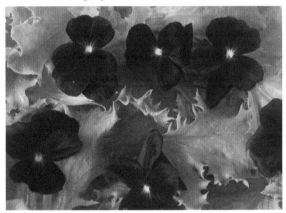

Chives & chive flowers for salads

Chives always liven up a salad, and their flowers are edible too. Once the flowers have finished, cut the whole plant down to an inch above the ground and you'll be rewarded with fresh new growth for summer salads and possibly more flowering, depending on the weather!

Lovage

Lovage is a bit like celery; you'll need space to grow this meaty herb. It's a hardy perennial herb, with growth dying down over winter and appearing again in spring. It has an intense celery flavour and can grow up to 6 feet (2m) high and about 3 feet (1m) wide (but should be considerably smaller if grown in a large pot or container). Its strong flavour makes it a wonderful herb for flavouring stews and soups and you can also use it to make pesto, using it instead of basil. It's almost impossible to buy in shops, so it's well worth growing your own.

Mustard leaves

I find mustard leaves can be very tasty in a salad, when mixed in with less powerful leaves such as lettuces and spinach. As the plant gets older and bigger, the leaves really do pack a punch, and if they become too hot for salads, they taste great in stir-fries. I always grow 'Red Giant' mustard leaf as it has such majestic purple-green leaves, as well as being very tasty, and 'Green in Snow' as the leaves are slightly milder with attractive crinkly serrated edges.

THIS MONTH'S LIST

JUNE

Despite even the rainiest of Junes, strawberries are ripening and sweet peas are perfuming the air. Lettuces and herbs sown in late February and March are filling the salad bowl and early potatoes should be ready for digging up. Sometimes, however, I find that my sowing doesn't always go to plan. This could be down to matters beyond my control such as poor quality seed that doesn't germinate or a bad batch of compost. If your first attempt at sowing seeds hasn't come to fruition, there's still time to have another go. Don't give up! It's warm enough now to sow seeds straight into the soil or growbags, but keep an eye out for marauding slugs, snails and mice.

As your plot bursts into productivity, it's a great time to visit other people's gardens for inspiration, particularly where there's mention of a kitchen garden or potager (and a nice piece of cake!).

Keep an eye on your crops as they grow and tie in climbing courgettes and tomatoes, feeding these hungry plants weekly with liquid seaweed and making sure they're well watered at all times to keep them healthy and to get the best yields.

COMMUNITY CORNER

With two community get-togethers already under our belt in March and May, and our vegetables beginning to grow, June is a good month to make time to start to apply for next year's funding. It helped us to form a constituted group to receive funds from our local council (see page 205), and photos taken during our get-togethers and of our glorious crops certainly helped to show potential funders what our project was all about.

Be realistic about your budget. What would you like to achieve? Buying seeds and growbags is our priority, but we also needed to budget for a van to deliver compost, shovels to load it and money for printing leaflets. Allow a bit extra for unexpected expenses. Taking part in Chelsea Fringe in May wasn't in our original plans for 2012, but having a little flexibility meant we could join the project with gusto and buy additional lettuce seeds to give away and clay to use for seed bomb-making.

Put aside some time to contact your local council to find out if they have any funds for community projects and how to apply for them. There are also national funding schemes, so search online to see if there are awarding bodies that could help fund your project.

Think of different ways to fundraise. Nicolette, David and Robert have formed a crack team of hedge trimmers. For a very reasonable fee they'll trim hedges in the neighbourhood, and funds go back into our scheme for more seeds and bulbs.

You could start up your own blog to record your activities, which will provide another great tool to illustrate your project to potential funders. 'My tiny plot' (www.mytinyplot.co.uk) is a great vegetable-growing gardening blog for small spaces and has a 'Build your own Blog' tutorial to help you get started. It's easy to follow and really does help you to get your own blog up and running. It's how I started mine.

While you get caught up with the paperwork, don't forget to give your vegetables some regular attention. Keep on watering and feeding with liquid seaweed to get the best out of your pots. Potatoes, tomatoes, runner beans, and strawberries will all be forming their fruit at this time of year, so make sure they get all the water they need to provide delicious plump produce. If you're growing blueberries in a pot, water them with rain water, as tap water is too alkaline for them.

Top right: Neighbours sharing strawberries
Bottom left: Julia and family on community plot
Bottom right: Mr Charalambous delivering spare fig tree
Previous page: Borage ice cubes, see Tip p113

🪴 SOWING & PLANTING 🪣

FLOWERS & FRUIT

Dead-heading flowers

It's really important to remove dead flower heads from both annuals and perennials, in order to prevent energy being diverted into seed production as this will stop plants producing new flowers.

The more you dead-head, the more flowers will be produced. If you want to have seeds from your plant for next year, just leave some of the flowers to form seed pods as the flowering period comes to an end.

Removing strawberry runners

Flowers on strawberries will be pollinated by bees, and will turn into delicious fruits over the next month or so. Just keep an eye on 'runners' forming at the same time. These are long thin stems coming from the parent plant that will start forming mini strawberry plants at their tips and developing roots as soon as they hit the ground. It's a great way to self-propagate, but you want all the plant's energy to be used for making fruit at the moment, so snip any runners off with secateurs as near to the base of the plant as possible. There'll be plenty of time to allow new runners to grow after all the strawberries have been eaten!

SEEDS TO SOW THIS MONTH
Outdoors: Peas and pea shoots, lettuces, spinach, beetroot, carrots, kohlrabi, courgettes and pumpkins, Swiss chard, sorrel, rocket, French and runner beans, leeks and nasturtiums.

Left: Dead-heading sweet peas

SIMPLE BUT BRILLIANT IDEAS

|||||||||||||||||||||||||||||||||||||||||||||||||||||||||||||||||||||||||||||||||||||||||

Netting over strawberries

I haven't played tennis for many years now. But I saw this wonderful netting support system (it could be cleverly marketed as such) at a friend's allotment and have been using it ever since to keep the birds off my fruit. Netting can be easily draped over tennis balls on bamboo canes (others use squash balls) and then taken off and stored when fruiting is over. Simple, but brilliant.

ONE POT SHOP

PEA SHOOTS
ANOTHER DELICIOUS (AND CHEAP!) EDIBLE CONTAINER IDEA

You will need:

1. Any container that's at least a few inches deep

2. Multi-purpose compost

3. Dried peas or leftover pea seeds

4. A watering can

5. An anti-squirrel device

Peas will usually grow up to 3 or 4 feet, but spare seeds can be planted now in a container and picked as delicious, quick-growing pea shoots to add to your salads. One sowing can be cropped two or even three times once the shoots are about 6 inches (15cm) tall.

If you don't have leftover pea seeds, try this idea (a much cheaper option), which comes from Mark at Vertical Veg (www.verticalveg.org.uk). Buy dried peas from your local grocery shop and soak overnight before planting. Neighbour Annie and I had a mini tasting session, comparing shoots grown from dried peas with shoots from pukka pea seeds. The result amazed us. We preferred the pea shoots grown from dried peas, which tasted much more pea-like.

STEP 1. Nearly fill a container with compost, leaving 1.5 inches (4cm) soil-free at the top. I used a wooden box left out as rubbish at our local shops, lined with an old compost bag punctured with holes.

STEP 2. Scatter seeds on top of the compost. You can sow them really close together, about half an inch (1cm) apart, as they are never going to grow into tall plants and you want to get as many shoots to eat as possible.

STEP 3. Cover the seeds with half an inch (1.5cm) of compost, and water in well with a fine rose on your watering can.

STEP 4. Cover with any device that will stop squirrels digging up all your freshly planted seeds. Peas will also take the fancy of slugs, snails and mice, so be vigilant! Leaves should appear in a week or so and shoots will be ready to crop in about three weeks. To harvest, nip them just above the lowest leaf and try not to eat straight away!

STEP 2

STEP 3

STEP 3

HARVESTING

Finally, after a couple of months of slim pickings, a whole heap of fruit and vegetables is ready to be harvested. Hurrah!

Lettuces

I love having lettuces in my front garden, crisp and fresh with no chemical sprays (unlike packs in the supermarket). Also, there are no wasted leaves left forgotten in the fridge. Always pick the outer leaves of the plant, rather than the whole lettuce, leaving inner leaves to carry on growing. This way, your lettuces will last a lot longer and supply you with fresh salads over the summer.

Carrots

Small 'Paris Market' carrots sown at the end of March and the beginning of April can now be pulled up for delicious bite-sized veg that children (and adults) love. Perfect for smaller containers and window boxes, they're a delight to harvest. Very sweet-tasting, too.

Strawberries

I've always grown strawberries. It seems like a crime not to. Nothing beats the taste of this fruit eaten while still warm on a sunny June day. Gluts do occur, and extra strawberries can easily be used to make pots of delicious home-made jam or outrageously indulgent puddings, such as Eton mess.

Kohlrabi

Kohlrabi has a sweet, cabbagy flavour, but it's much more juicy than its cabbagy cousins. It can be picked when it's the size of a (slightly squashed) tennis ball. And it's great for grating or cutting finely into salads; it can also be steamed or stir-fried. The leaves are edible and can be eaten like spinach, although they have a slightly thicker leaf.

Parsley

Parsley happily grows in pots, but make sure you keep it well watered. Perfect for livening up a salad giving it a fresh herby taste, and delicious in all sorts of sauces.

Early potatoes

'Sharpe's Express' is a heritage variety over 100 years old, but popular because it has a really good flavour. It doesn't crop as heavily as others, such as 'Foremost', but it has a more floury texture than lots of other earlies, so a really good all-rounder for boiling, steaming and roasting.

African basil leaves

A perennial plant, sadly it's not very hardy and if it's to survive winter, it will need to be brought inside before the first frosts. However, it's worth pampering as its leaves are very decorative and its taste is truly delicious, having a slightly coarser texture than its European relatives. Like any basil plant, it's great as a flavouring for salads, pizzas and pasta sauces and perfect for adding to ricotta cheese when stuffing courgette flowers. A must-have herb for any window sill or balcony.

Edible flowers

Orange or red nasturtiums have a lovely strong peppery crunch to them, borage has a slight cucumber flavour to match its cool blue looks, while pansies add a soft velvety texture to the mix.

TIP Borage flowers can be frozen in ice cubes to grace any summer cocktail, and look especially gorgeous in a fruity glass of Pimms. Pick the borage flowers and carefully prise them away from their hairy backing before adding to an ice tray.

Left: Borage growing in the front garden

THIS MONTH'S LIST

JULY

If you've had a reasonably warm summer, your growbags should be overrun with runner beans and French beans. However, if it's been cool and rainy, bean and tomato flowers will be reluctantly starting to bloom (cross your fingers that the bees will be out in sufficient numbers to pollinate your crops). Wildflowers not only attract bees, but offer a rural escape from urban life. Over the last few years, we've planted several different annual native wildflower seed mixes in our tree pits. Although they've looked fantastic, by the end of June or July most of the blooms are over. By adding some non-native flowers into their blends, wildflower specialists Pictorial Meadows have created mixes that will perform well into autumn. Their 'Candy Mix' seeds, for example, which we sowed at the beginning of April, are looking delightful, with clusters of delicate snapdragon-like flowers.

⌂ COMMUNITY CORNER ⌐

With a bit of luck you'll be spending all your free (gardening) time outdoors, as will your neighbours. It's amazing to see what everyone is growing and to savour home-grown vegetables in salads, perhaps even try out a few new recipes. Charlotte says, 'Being part of the community growing project has been a fantastic experience for many reasons. As a keen gardener, but one who always grows the same thing year on year, the free seeds have made me try growing lots of new things. Most importantly, it's created a community where people stop and talk and get to know each other.' The summer presents plenty of opportunities to have a good natter with neighbours and hear their stories. Some people have lived in our streets for over 50 years. We live just down the road from the old Arsenal football stadium and Lily can remember a man sitting in a hut in his front garden (which has since been built on), selling kindling wood on match days for coal fires.

As crops are ready to harvest, make sure that you take plenty of photos for future funding. In between picking vegetables and chatting with neighbours, continue funding applications and planning for next year. See what's grown best in your growbags, ask what neighbours would like to try out next year and start gathering information together for ordering seeds for next spring.

Don't let up on the watering, especially if temperatures start to soar. Pots and containers have no access to water in the ground so unless it's raining, water pots every day and twice a day for small pots (in my case, teapots and colanders) on really hot days. Having a water butt installed in our community plot has made a huge difference to our water supplies. I'd highly recommend it. Not only does it avoid using mains water, but rainwater is actually better for plants that prefer acid soils such as blueberries (and azaleas and camellias). Manuel has devised his own fantastic rain-collecting system, with 12 interconnected plastic rubbish bins holding enough water to keep all his plants well watered throughout any drought. Bravo, Manuel.

Top left: Children pricking out seedlings
Top right: Lily and her growbag
Bottom: Manuel with his water system
Previous page: Multi-coloured fairy toadflax
alongside an orange Californian poppy

SOWING & PLANTING

VEGETABLES

Water tomatoes regularly to avoid blossom end rot

Tomatoes are the divas of the vegetable world and need pampering. Blossom end rot isn't a disease like tomato blight but the hardening at the bottom of the tomato will still make your fruit inedible. The best way to prevent this happening is by watering regularly and trying not to let the soil dry out. Fine in theory, but not many of us are around to water two or three times a day during hot weather. So water as much and as regularly as you can, and place trays under pots to stop the soil from drying out. Also, never use growbags to plant in, as the soil is too shallow for the roots. Grow in big pots instead (see page 91).

As soon as you harvest your vegetables, sow again

While you are harvesting your crops, take advantage of the space that becomes available and carry on sowing vegetables that will take you into autumn. Harvested potatoes will leave a large pot where runner beans, carrots, beetroot or kohlrabi can be planted. Small carrots in window boxes can be replaced by cut-and-come-again lettuces or rocket. Lettuces will happily grow from seed now, but note that seeds will not germinate when temperatures are above 25 degrees Centigrade. Sow lettuce seeds late in the afternoon as temperatures start to cool and position the pot in the shade. If you already have some spare seedlings in modules, use these to fill gaps in planters and pots.

Leeks – there's still time to plant out seedlings

If you grew leeks from seed earlier in the year, you may have a few seedlings still waiting to be planted out. Again, any spare spot you see, pop a leek in! (see page 74). They're a handsome vegetable and will look good growing among flowers and other veg.

SEEDS TO SOW THIS MONTH
Outdoors: Lettuces, carrots, rocket, courgettes, French and runner beans, kohlrabi, mustard leaves, chervil, coriander, beetroot, sugar snap peas and pea shoots

Left: Nikki sowing seeds in her growbag

SOWING & PLANTING
FRUIT

Strawberries – new plants for free – it's easy!

Strawberries crop best in their second and third years, and then yields will sadly start to wane. After the third or fourth year, it's best to replace your plants. What's great, however, is that you can start growing your next generation of plants as soon as your strawberries have finished fruiting.

Strawberries throw out runners, long thin stems, from the mother plant all summer long and once they touch the soil, they'll start to sprout roots and grow into new plants.

If you let runners run amok in soil, you'll eventually have an overcrowded strawberry patch with plants competing for light and nutrients. In pots, on the other hand, the runners will hang over the edge with nowhere to root into.

A great solution for both scenarios is to peg down runners into new small pots. I normally use a piece of garden wire bent over into a large U shape and push the wire over the runner into the soil, so that the runner makes contact with the soil. Magically, roots will start to grow and new plants will be formed. Keep the runner attached to the mother plant for six to eight weeks, then when the runner is looking strong and healthy, cut it from the mother plant to give it its independence. Once plants have developed a good root system, put them in a larger pot or a new strawberry bed (see page 137). Next summer you will get a small crop, but the following two years, your fruits will arrive in full force.

Top: Small strawberry runners being grown in pots
Bottom: Pegging down a runner with wire into a pot

SIMPLE BUT BRILLIANT IDEAS

|||||||||||||||||||||||||||||||||||||||||||||||||||||||||||||||||||||||||||

Garden sculpture

You can't help but be inspired when you visit Lucy MacKenzie's Lip na Cloiche garden on Mull. Found objects (anything from cast-iron bedheads to teapots) are transformed into sculptural installations throughout the gardens, shifting the everyday into something quite extraordinary. If you're ever near Mull, it's a must to visit! The planting will amaze you too. To see more of this splendidly quirky garden, have a look at http://outofmyshed.co.uk/2012/04/20/inspiration-at-lip-na-cloiche/

ONE POT SHOP

PLANTING UP A PERENNIAL MEDITERRANEAN HERB BASKET

You will need:

1. An old basket (I've used a large basket from the front of a disused bike)

2. An old plastic compost bag for lining

3. Crock and 4 or 5 good handfuls of horticultural grit

4. John Innes no.2 compost. As perennial plants, your herbs will be in this basket for a few years, so use a soil-based compost rather than a multi-purpose one as it won't dry out as quickly and it will be better at holding onto nutrients

5. Small pots of herbs: here we've used two pots of marjoram and three small lavender plants, but you could also use oregano or sage or all four together.

STEP 1. Keeping the plants in their pots, soak for about 10-15 minutes in the sink or a bucket of water before planting.

STEP 2. Baskets are a little too loose a weave to hold compost on their own, so line your basket with an old plastic compost bag and put four or five holes in the bottom of the plastic so that water can drain out easily. This should also stop the basket from rotting so quickly.

STEP 3. Add crock to the bottom of the bag/basket, then fill with compost until two-thirds full, and finally pour in four or five handfuls of grit and mix in really well. Mediterranean herbs don't like sitting in wet soil, especially in winter, and this provides extra drainage.

STEP 4. Position herbs before you start planting to see that they fit in the basket with gaps of a good few inches (7-10cm) in between plants, as they will need space to grow into.

STEP 5. Take the plants out of the pots and scratch out the roots if they look pot-bound. Then plant into the basket, adding extra soil around them just to the level that they were originally planted in their pots.

STEP 6. Water in well.

STEP 1

STEP 2

STEP 3

STEP 4

STEP 5

STEP 5

STEP 6

Wow! What a month for harvesting! If you can't eat your abundance of courgettes and beans, knock on doors and share some of your crops with neighbours.

Sugar snap 'Sugar Ann' peas

These deliciously sweet sugar snap peas can be eaten raw, steamed or added to a stir-fry. The 'Sugar Ann' variety is a dwarf pea, only growing to about 18 inches. It needs no supports, so is ideal for growing in containers and planters. There's still time to plant another batch to harvest in September.

Runner beans

Runner beans are a taste of my childhood and a great taste of summer. You wait for them for months, and then they tend to come all at once. There are many ways to cook them. A light steam then served with a knob of butter is still my preferred method, but beans cooked with tomatoes and garlic is also a rather delicious option.

Lettuces

Sow different lettuces every three to four weeks and you'll have plenty of leaves all summer long. I start my seeds off in modules, so that whenever there is a gap in a window box or in one of my raised beds, small plants can be popped in, which will be ready to eat in a few weeks.

Right: Manuel and his runner beans
Below: Mixed lettuce leaves

'Chioggia' beetroot

'Chioggia' beetroot looks fairly non-descript from the outside, but cut it open and its stripy psychedelic gorgeousness is revealed as a mini work of art. Sadly, the markings fade when cooked, but eaten raw, sliced nice and thinly, the stripes will make a decorative addition to any salad.

Courgette 'Soleil'

This yellow courgette is wonderfully decorative in salads and stir-fries. The plant is lovely and compact so great for a large container or growing directly in the ground. Its dazzling flowers and fruit light up any sunny front garden throughout July and August.

'Tromboncino' courgette

This is a wild beast of a courgette, clambering up miles of bamboo canes. You'll need to snip the top growth off when you can no longer reach to tie in its stems, or tie it horizontally along a washing line (or something similar) so it has more space to grow.

Sweet peas

I can't imagine a veg patch without sweet peas. With their delicate blooms, they are the fragrance of summer days. My first batch sown in February tends to flower in June and my second sowing in April then flowers all through July. (See page 41 for how to sow and my favourite varieties.)

Left: 'Chioggia' beetroot
Above: Eleni cutting 'Tromboncino' courgettes

Japanese wineberries

Japanese wineberries (*Rubus phoenicolasius*) perfectly fill the fruit gap in between summer and autumn fruiting raspberries, cropping from late July and into August. They're sweet, very juicy, with a slightly sharp, peppery aftertaste. They look like small raspberries, but glossier in appearance and grow in clusters along elegant pinkish, furry-looking, slightly spiky stems. They can grow into enormous rambling plants, but can be artfully trained along wires or bamboo canes to grow in smaller spaces. Green berries are revealed next to other ripening berries as if venturing out of an alien's pod.

Curly kale

Spring sowings of Kale are ready for picking now and over summer, but will be going to seed come autumn. Sow more seeds now (be it Cavalo nero, red or curly kale) and you'll have these beautiful leaves throughout autumn and winter when vegetable pickings are thinner. Their decorative and sculptural presence will also be a highlight in the winter garden.

'Foremost' early potatoes

This is a reliable early variety, producing great yields. If you don't have any ground to plant in, plan on using growbags next year.

Rhubarb

Some varieties of rhubarb, such as 'Brandy Carr Scarlet', can be harvested right into September; while in years when the weather has been rather cool, 'Timperley Early' has still been still producing fresh tasty stems in July.

Right: Matt picking curly kale in his front garden growbeds

THIS MONTH'S LIST

AUGUST

The sun is shining and it's hard to imagine that autumn (and dare I say it, winter,) is just around the corner. Crops such as French beans, beetroot, carrots and delicious leaves are filling your plate, but now is the time to plan seriously again and sow more seeds for autumn and winter harvesting. Take stock of what has worked over the past few months and what you really enjoyed eating.

Leaves and herbs that may have bolted in hotter weather such as spinach, coriander, Swiss chard and mustard leaves are ideal candidates to sow now and will survive even the toughest of winters. Try sowing in August and into September some of the hardier lettuces, such as the butterhead varieties 'Arctic King', 'Valdor' and 'Marvel of Four Seasons', to see if they can survive winter in your front garden. Gardening friend Valerie recommends 'Winter Density', which is like a large 'Little Gem', as it survives all but the hardest of frosts in Sheffield. My mum says she can harvest 'Lamb's lettuce' right up until Christmas. Pickings will be much slimmer than in summer, but it's such a treat to have salads later in the year that it's worth having a go.

If you missed the opportunity earlier in the year to sow other hardy vegetables such as kale, you'll still be able to order small plants from all the major seed suppliers and some garden centres.

Everyone is proud of what they've achieved and it's great to have the opportunity to catch up with neighbours as we document the year's harvest. I regularly update our blog page (www.outofmyshed.co.uk/btg) with images, so that others can see what our project is all about and how it continues to flourish and grow.

If you haven't applied for funding, start doing so now. Contact your local council to see if there's any funding for community groups or google national awarding bodies. Local councillors have their own individual spending pots (around £6,000 in Islington in 2012) to spend on their ward, so it's worth approaching them for funds to help green up your area. Ask around and see if one of your neighbours has a talent for filling out funding application forms.

If you've formed a constituted group, you'll need to have a committee meeting to sign off your accounts before reapplying for funding.

Again, this sounds more daunting than it actually is. We have a core of six neighbours (the committee) that meet two or three times a year over a cup of coffee in someone's kitchen. We chat about successes and failures, sign off the year's expenses and brainstorm; it's a great time to plan for the year ahead.

As you pop out to the shops, you catch up with families excitedly digging up their potato crop or other neighbours picking runner beans for dinner. If you're going on holiday, it's worth asking one of your veg-growing neighbours to keep an eye on your plants. It's heartbreaking to come back from holiday to find that your tenderly nurtured plants have suffered, especially if there's been scorching weather. Try the 'Paddling pool holiday watering system' on page 78. It works.

Top left: Eleni with her French and runner beans
Top right: Charlotte and her front garden potatoes
Bottom left: Naomi picking French beans
Bottom right: Liesbet with her squash in generous planters

Plant up strawberry runners

Every three years or so, you'll need to replace your old strawberries as the amount of fruit diminishes. Strawberries do best in full sun, so bear this in mind when creating a new bed. In their second year of growth, start to plant up a new bed or new pots, with runners that have developed a good root system (see page 121). These new plants can replace the old plants, after they've fruited, next summer. It's best not to use the old strawberry beds or the old compost in your pots, as this will encourage a build-up of pests and diseases, and besides, these two beds (and extra pots) will be growing simultaneously for a year or so. If you don't have any room to create another bed right now, keep the runners in pots until more space becomes available and pot them on if they start to outgrow their current container. If you haven't grown your own runners, have a look at page 52 on exciting strawberries to order and a list of suppliers. These small plants will be sent out in late summer or in March'

Planting strawberries in the soil

Mix plenty of garden compost, well-rotted manure or shop-bought compost into the soil before planting, as strawberries need rich soil. They also need plenty of space to produce good fruit, so allow at least 15 inches (38cm) between plants and plant rows 18 inches (45cm) apart. Plant the strawberries so that they are at the same level in the soil as they were in the pots and water in well. Keep them well watered as they settle in, being especially vigilant in hot weather.

Planting strawberries in pots and growbags

I've never really got on with planting strawberries in traditional strawberry pots (with lots of different holes), as I've found it difficult to make sure all the plants get fed and watered well. I prefer giving each plant its own reasonably sized pot (at least 9 inches in diameter). You could also use a large planter, like an old wooden wine box or a Marshalls growbed, to grow a number of plants together. This way, the plants get as many nutrients and as much water as they need, which will ensure an abundant crop come next summer. Use John Innes no.3 compost or good garden compost – not multi–purpose compost – as these plants need good rich soil to produce great berries.

Left: Strawberries growing in a bed
Above: Small strawberry runners in pots

SIMPLE BUT BRILLIANT IDEAS

||||||||||||||||||||||||||||||||||||||||||||||||||||||||||||||||||||||||||||||

Plantlock to keep your bikes safe

These 'Plantlocks' are made by the Front Yard Company in Kentish Town in London (www.frontyardcompany.co.uk) and I must say, look rather fetching even without a bike attached! Fill these large metal containers (available in red or green) with sunflowers, mini wildflower meadows and great veg. Immovable once filled with soil and plants, this fab invention retails at £135 (in 2012) and seems to be just the ticket for your urban bike storage needs. I love this one packed with herbs.

ONE POT SHOP

A SUITCASE OF WINTER VEGETABLES

Use the largest container or pot you can find as Swiss chard is a meaty plant, and the more space it has, the bigger it will grow.

You will need:

1. A small seed tray (or any small plastic container at least 2 or 3 inches deep)

2. Multi-purpose compost for seed tray and John Innes no.2, home-made or council recycled compost for the larger container

3. A large pot or a large container – I've used an old suitcase

4. Crock

5. Swiss chard seeds. Sow 'Bright Lights' for a great mix, with stems producing vibrant colours, or 'Ruby'

STEP 1. Almost fill the seed tray, leaving an inch soil-free at the top.

STEP 2. Water the soil first with a watering can.

STEP 3. Sow the seeds thinly, about an inch or so apart.

STEP 4. Cover the seeds with half an inch of compost, water again.

STEP 5. After about a week to 10 days, seedlings will appear and in about three weeks, they will be ready to pot on into the large container.

STEP 6. Place the crock at the bottom of the large container and almost fill with compost. Transplant the seedlings, positioning them 9 inches (23cm) apart as they need plenty of room to grow into large plants. You could also plant just one seedling in an individual pot, at least eight inches (20cm) in diameter.

STEP 7. Water in well.

August is another month of plenty, when all your hard work is rewarded with delicious tastes and flavours. However, don't rest on your laurels! As you free up pots, sow more seeds and seedlings for cropping in autumn and winter – the aim is to have fresh vegetables all year round.

Spinach

One of my all-time favourite vegetables. Young leaves are a useful addition to salads and larger leaves are great either steamed or boiled. Not a fancy veg, but a great staple and one that will see you all through winter if sown again in August.

French beans

French beans have been great performers as part of our veg-growing scheme. Both the pink flowers and purple fruit are wonderfully decorative. Sadly, the purple turns to green as soon as they start to cook, but they taste fantastic and are a good-value plant as crops keep on coming for weeks.

Tree spinach

Tree spinach is a marvel. A close relation of 'Fat Hen' and 'Good King Henry' (all in the *Chenopodium* family), this tall bushy plant (growing up to 6 feet/2m) is great for decoration and for its edible leaves. The bright pink dusting on the smaller leaves makes them a sparkling addition to any salad and the larger leaves can be cooked as spinach; however, unlike most spinach varieties, these greens won't shrink to a fraction of their original size. Serve with a drizzle of olive oil and a squeeze of lemon.

'Charlotte' potatoes

These, left, are the 'Charlotte' potatoes which I grew on top of grass, with no digging (see page 55) They've grown well, giving a very respectable yield of 15lb (6.7kg) from just three seed potatoes. If you have a spare bit of sunny ground, have a go at these next year. You may well be converted to the "no dig' growing system.

Sunflowers

Sunflowers are one of the most joyous flowers around and planted en masse create a stunning display. All this from just a few seeds planted in April! Bees love them and birds (and pesky squirrels) will feed on the seed heads well into autumn.

Left: Unearthing 'Charlotte' potatoes
Below: Summer salad with edible flowers

Hollyhocks

Hollyhocks (and all members of the Mallow family) are edible. Hollyhocks have quite substantial flowers, so gently rip them into bite-size pieces, and add to salads for gorgeous decoration. Hollyhocks are biennial plants, which means that they produce lots of leaves in the first year of growth and flower the following year. If you buy and plant small plants now, they should flower next summer and for a few years after that.

Lettuces

Mix them with edible flowers for a real showstopper. I grow in batches every few weeks from late February up until September, so that I can have home-grown leaves for most of the year. Sow another batch now for more autumn leaves.

Pea shoots

Sown in mid-July, these shoots will be ready to eat just three weeks later. I always find it difficult not to eat them as I pick; consequently my husband doesn't see many of them in the salad bowl. Grow plenty and sow often (see page 108) and these fresh tips will delight you all summer long. Harvest when 4 to 6 inches (10-15cm) tall, picking them just above the lowest leaf, and leave the stems to regrow for another picking later in the month. Pealicious.

'Tromboncino' courgettes

'Tromboncino' courgettes, unlike their softer cousins, don't have any seeds but are a solid mass when you cut into them. They are not the best courgettes for flavour, but can work really well when thinly sliced and cooked with fried purple onions and tomatoes and flavoured with sweet marjoram. My friend Lisette grates them into long strands and after boiling for a minute, eats them with a sauce, just like pasta.

French tarragon

French tarragon is a delicious herb with a mild aniseed flavour, much admired by chefs. I love using it when I'm cooking chicken. A tender perennial, it will die if left outside over winter. Even indoors, the plant will stop producing over winter, but will pick up again come spring.

THIS MONTH'S LIST

SEPTEMBER

Days are getting shorter and nights are drawing in. You'll start to feel that the end of the growing season is upon you. However, there are still seeds to sow and harvests to crop and, as the busier months in the garden are over, this is a good time to take stock and think about what to grow next year.

There are some years when my successional lettuce sowing hasn't always gone perfectly to plan; batches of new seedlings disappear overnight, the culprits leaving slimy trails. However, trying alternative quick-growing leaves for salads, such as pea shoots, has been a revelation. I've been amazed, for example, by the success of my potted autumn raspberries. It's just a matter of space and time, trying to squeeze all these pots into the front garden and window ledges.

Nurseries these days offer tomato (and chilli) tasting days. If you can get to one, it's a fantastic opportunity to sample all sorts of tomatoes that you may not have had the chance to grow yet. Specialist growers offer a wealth of knowledge, so don't be afraid to ask questions, especially if you've had some problems with your plants this year, and pick up great growing tips for future tomato production! While you're there, see what other exciting fruit and vegetable plants the nursery grows and add some of these to your growing list for the year ahead.

🏠 COMMUNITY CORNER ⚚

It's a good time to put heads together and start planning for an autumn Cake Sunday. Ask around for willing cake makers (you'll be surprised at the number of experts you have in your midst) and think about what you could give away for planting in autumn.

Daffodil bulbs have given us glorious early blooms in spring, so funds permitting, we now order a whole heap of bulbs to share out at our October gathering. Dwarf varieties such as 'Tete a Tete' and 'Minnow' look wonderful in window boxes and they can be whipped out when they've finished flowering and replaced by gorgeous edible plants. Equally, larger varieties of daffodils in pots, such as the bold 'Dutch Master', will give a dazzling golden display come March, and why not try the delicate white 'Poeticus' varieties, which will continue flowering into April and May?

If you have a spare piece of unloved ground in your neighbourhood, have a go at planting a bold mix of daffodil, crocus or tulip bulbs to create a dazzling display in the spring (see page 153). Simone, a neighbour who doesn't have her own garden, emailed us to say, 'I just wanted to thank you for spearheading the urban gardens/bloom competition. I have watched with great interest and joy as various bits of wildflower gardens have popped up in the area and it's lovely to see all the beautiful colours. I don't have a garden or access to a terrace but I love what you're doing.'

Top left: Gary picking his runner beans
Top right: Ellie and daughter watering rocket
Bottom left: Colin tying in 'Red Mini Turban' squashes
Bottom right: Daffodil bulbs planted now will reap the benefits come March

SOWING & PLANTING
FLOWERS & FRUIT

Ordering bulbs for spring flowering

Every year I have great fun experimenting with planting bulbs in pots as well as in my garden. They're great for giving bees an early source of nectar and they supply such a joyous splash of colour. Crocuses will look amazing in February, growing in window boxes, pots and or emerging through grass. Once planted, they'll come back year after year, building up into big clumps of rich purples and sumptuous yellows.

Daffodils (*Narcissi*) bulbs come in lots of different sizes – from the miniature through to whoppers such as 'Red Devon'. I buy most of my spring bulbs from Peter Nyssen (www.peternyssen.com) who have a great website for helping you choose the right variety. They list the flowers' height, whether they are scented and also importantly, when your bulbs will flower. If you plan it right (and the weather is obliging), you can have daffodils in bloom from February until the end of May.

Daffodil bulbs can be planted from September to build up good roots before the weather turns cold. Although not recommended, I have planted daffodils as late as the beginning of December and have been lucky to get great flowering the following spring. If bulbs still look viable – not dried out or squashy and mouldy, then give them a try. It's always good to experiment.

Tulips are my favourite spring bulbs. Order now, plant in November and you'll be rewarded with a display that will lift your soul come springtime. There are 15 different shapes of tulip with an abundant array of colours within each shape. Take note of the height and month when they flower if you want a mixture of bulbs to work well together and flower at the same time.

Pruning Japanese wineberries

After you have eaten all your berries for this year, you'll need to cut back the stems that bore the fruit. There will also be new stems that grew during this year and haven't produced fruit yet, but don't prune them, as your fruit will grow on these stems next year. Once you have cut back the old stems (approximately half of the plant), tie in your new stems and look forward to more of these gorgeous berries next summer.

SEEDS TO SOW THIS MONTH
Outdoors: Lettuces, mustard leaves, spinach, chard, pea shoots, chervil, coriander, winter purslane, rocket

Left: Orange tulip 'Ballerina' with pink 'Curly Sue' alongside 'Red Giant Mustard Leaf' and orange ranunculus in my front garden raised bed

SIMPLE BUT BRILLIANT IDEAS

||||||||||||||||||||||||||||||||||||||||||||||||||||||||||||||||||||||||||||||||||||||||||||||||||

Anti-squirrel device

After years of squirrels digging up my freshly planted pots, I have built some mini cages to fit on top of old wine boxes so that I can still grow salad leaves by the front door. As soon as the plants are of a decent size and can look after themselves, I remove the cages and keep them for use on my next sowings. The cages are simple to make. All you need is some chicken wire, nails and eight small pieces of thin wood (these were reclaimed from a nearby skip). First, nail the base pieces of wood together in a rectangle to fit around the wooden box, then nail on the four upright pieces. Shape and position the wire around the wooden framework, tying in with small pieces of wire, and then nail the wire onto the base. A staple gun makes life a lot easier.

ONE POT SHOP

ROCKET IN A POT

Having harvested my early carrots, I now have a lovely container (see red bucket, right) in which to sow something else in September. Rocket will germinate in three or four days at this time of year – very gratifying to see your efforts so swiftly rewarded. Sow your seeds fairly thickly and 10 days later, the first thinnings from the pot will be ready to grace your salad bowl.

You will need:
1. Your recycled container **2.** Fresh multi-purpose compost **3.** Rocket seeds

STEP 1. Almost refill the bucket leaving an inch free of soil at the top of the bucket.

STEP 2. Scatter the rocket seeds fairly thickly (close together) as you can use the thinnings as tiny leaves to add to your salads.

STEP 3. Cover seeds with half an inch of compost.

STEP 4. Water in well, and keep well watered as the seedlings grow.

STEP 5. After 10 days or so, start thinning the seedlings out (see page 202). Carry on thinning out evenly as the seedlings get bigger, until there are only four or five plants that are left growing.

September should be providing you with an abundance of crops ready to harvest. Carrots and beetroots can be pulled out of the ground, and there may even be pickings from later rhubarb varieties such as 'Brandy Carr Scarlet'. Long-awaited crops such as tomatoes and autumn raspberries should also be turning temptingly ripe throughout the month.

'Pink Fir Apple' potatoes

These gnarly tubers are another delightful seasonal treat, and relatively rare in shops as they're a late-crop salad potato. This is one worth growing every year. With its nutty flavour, and waxy texture, it is unique and makes a delicious addition to any meal.

Squash

Squashes can be too boisterous for small growing spaces, but there are some very tempting mini squashes out there that will climb acrobatically (with a little bit of tying in), using supports. They struggle in cooler summers, but when they perform at their best, they're joyously decorative as well as being edible.

'Arran Victory' potatoes

These potatoes come with a past. They were named in 1918 to celebrate the end of the First World War. They have a dry, pulpy rather than waxy texture, which rules them out for boiling, but they make the most delicious roast potatoes. I'm never quite sure if I want to use my precious growing space for main-crop varieties, but digging these purple tubers out of the ground makes my heart sing, so I find a space to squeeze them in most years.

Right: 'Mini Red Turban' squash

More pea shoots

Keep sowing these every week or so, and you'll have bucketfuls of succulent shoots for salads and stir-fries.

Autumn-fruiting raspberries

Raspberries never taste so sweet as when eased from their cores on a warm sunny day. As summer turns into autumn, fresh raspberries are a real luxury, as most other soft fruits are finished for the year. Enjoy your juicy pickings, and with a mild autumn, you could even be cropping until Christmas.

Spinach & rocket thinnings

You can enjoy these succulent mini leaves in salads. They're so fresh and sweet that I often sow a few more seeds than I need, just to be able to eat the thinnings.

'Mara des Bois' strawberries

I can't figure out why more people don't grow these 'Mara des Bois' strawberries (available from www.pomonafruits.co.uk). They're a cross between wild and cultivated strawberries, which supply you continuously with delicious medium-sized fruits from July until October. Achingly sweet and sumptuously juicy, they are a must-have for strawberry lovers.

Tomatoes

Tomatoes have finally arrived. One taste of your deliciously sweet, home-grown crop, and you realise why we bother to grow this rather challenging vegetable. If you love the variety you've grown, keep one ripe tomato to collect seeds from, as seeds will be viable for up to 10 years. (Victoriana Nursery have a great 'how to collect tomato seeds' video on YouTube). As your tomatoes start to ripen, it is also as well to leave a ripe tomato or two on the vine; these will give off a gas called ethylene, which will help the rest of the tomatoes to ripen.

Carrots

Growing in buckets may not provide you with huge winter stores of this root veg, but the joy of pulling carrots equals that of digging up your home-grown potatoes. They're beautifully sweet due to a very high sugar content, and this 'Rainbow Mix' picured left is a gorgeous sight to behold (available from www.pennardplants.com). They retain their colours when cooked and the purple carrots are stunning with a contrasting orange interior. If you like good-looking food, then add 'Cosmic Purple' (available from www.chilternseeds.co.uk) to your seed list for next year.

Lettuces

Small trays of living lettuces from supermarkets can be divided up and will do really well potted on into all sorts of containers. The more petite the container, the more watering it will need, but I love the look of these wavy oakleaf lettuces in a formal teapot to the right.

Right: Colin picking lettuces

THIS MONTH'S LIST

OCTOBER

You can really feel the chill in the air and while salad and mustard leaves are still growing, yields are getting smaller. I'm passionate about seasonal crops and this is when your winter vegetables come into their own. Summer sowings of carrots and beetroots can be harvested as well as leeks sown in April and May. If you haven't grown these vegetables this year but like the idea of this autumn feast, then start adding them to your seed list for next spring.

Every October, I get very excited about digging up my first crop of Jerusalem artichokes (see harvesting section on page 174); has it really been six months since they were last available?

Some years, October is all woolly hats and scarves, while others are so mild that it feels as if they're just an extension of the summer. If you find yourself in a mild year and have a pot or a little bit of growing space to spare, experiment with sowing a few different mustard leaves at the beginning of October, such as 'Mibuna', 'Mizuna', 'Green in Snow', 'Green Frills', 'Red Knight Mizuna' or 'Red Giant'. These hardy plants should have just enough time to grow before the harsher weather arrives and will give you a delicious spicy treat during the depths of winter. Mix the reds and greens together and they'll also give you a decorative container or patch in the garden.

🏠 COMMUNITY CORNER 🛒

By now we're all spending much more time indoors, but it's still good to meet up in Manuel's front garden for another Cake Sunday, to catch up after summer and to give away bulbs. Despite the cooler weather, it seems that neighbours still have an appetite to get together. It's lovely to get feedback and hear how our project touches people's lives. Manuel comments that as people get to know one another, and look out for each other, it makes him feel that the area is a safer place to live. Lily's daughter Jennifer emails to tell me of her mother's delight at having successfully grown French beans and corn in our experimental 'Three Sisters' growing project, following Native American vegetable-growing practices in our growbags.

Other neighbours express the same sentiment: Bernd said, 'The project inspired me to grow my own strawberries in the front garden and I was amazed how sweet and delicious they were. After years of buying strawberries from supermarkets I had totally forgotten how flavourful they can be. However, the biggest impact of the project is the transformation of a neighbourhood into a community where people greet each other and stop on the street for a small chat.'

Annie rates the project for the way that 'Neighbours stop, chat, laugh and get to know each other in a spontaneous and natural way that used to happen in a bygone era when our lives were not so hectic. I love wandering slowly up the road now to soak in what each garden is growing.'

I second that. Since getting involved with the vegetable-growing project, I feel part of the community more than ever and enjoy seeing familiar faces when I'm in my front garden or just nipping out to the local shops.

I'm greeted by the smell of ripening tomatoes, cascades of purple beans, artichoke screens six feet high, vintage suitcases loaded with veg under front windows, wine boxes stuffed with herbs on window sills, colourful tins crammed with nasturtiums and tree pits crammed to overflowing with wildflowers and plants – our very own little oasis in the middle of the urban jungle.

Top left: Annie and Mrs. Tsioupra
Top right: Cakes galore at Cake Sunday
Bottom left: Collecting bulbs at Cake Sunday
Bottom right: Eugenie growing French beans

Planting daffodil bulbs directly into the soil or into grass

As well as thriving when planted directly into the soil, lots of bulbs will grow well through grass. This is called naturalising. Catalogues and websites often highlight bulbs that are good for naturalising, but if you're not sure, then give the bulb supplier a ring before you make your order.

Planting in soil If you're planting directly into the soil, scatter bulbs around in a random (-ish) fashion before you plant, to give a less regimented look. The should be very roughly 3 inches (7.5cm) apart as they will clump up over the years, and as a rule of thumb, they should be planted to approximately three times their depth. Dig a hole to the correct depth for your size of bulb, pop it in the hole with the roots at the bottom and the narrow neck at the top and then cover with soil. Firm down the soil with your hands and water in well.

Planting in grass If you're going to plant in a grassed area and have a large number of bulbs to plant, then it's a good idea (and quicker!) to plant in clumps.

To do this:

STEP 1. Mark out your area using carefully scattered flour or some chalk spray.

STEP 2. Define the area using the sharp edge of a spade.

STEP 3. Remove the turf with the spade, being careful to not to disturb the grass roots too much by taking out a chunky slice of soil 3-4 inches (7.5-10cm) in depth along with the grass.

STEP 4. Dig out the soil to the right depth that your bulb needs (remember: around three times the depth of the bulbs).

STEP 5. Plant bulbs in the hole with the roots at the bottom and narrow neck at the top, placing them 2 to 3 inches (5-7.5cm) apart.

STEP 6. Finally, replace the soil and the grass on top of the bulbs, then tread in the grass so that the roots make contact with the soil beneath.

STEP 7. Water in well. Your efforts will be gloriously rewarded come March and April.

SIMPLE BUT BRILLIANT IDEAS

||||||||||||||||||||||||||||||||||||||||||||||||||||||||||||||||||||||||||||||||||||||||||||

Allotments & alternative growing spaces

If you're lucky enough to live in an area where spaces are available, allotments are a great way to expand your growing experiments and meet other like-minded growers. You'll need time and commitment, but the rewards are great. All is not lost if allotments are unavailable. When someone commented on my blog about their frustration at not having a garden, it prompted me to think that urban dwellers, and indeed anyone without their own outside space, must seize the initiative. If you see an unused front garden, why not knock on the door and ask if you can use the space to grow veg and flowers? Sharing growing spaces with neighbours can only improve life for everyone.

ONE POT SHOP

TULIPS IN A POT

If I only had room for one pot of spring flowers, I would plump for tulips. They sing out in April and May when most other flowers have yet to appear. I tend to plant tulips towards the end of October as the weather starts to cool but I have even planted them as late as the end of December. I plant my tulip bulbs in layers to pack in as many as I can for a great spring display, and you can use the same method for planting daffodils in pots. (See page 153 for ordering bulbs.)

You will need:

1. Tulip bulbs. Either use one variety or mix colours for a dazzling display. Make sure you choose bulbs that will grow to about the same height and will flower at the same time, as different varieties can flower in different months

2. A large terracotta or plastic pot at least 10 inches (25cm) deep

3. Crock for drainage

4. 'Multi-purpose compost'

STEP 1. Add some crock into the bottom of your pot for drainage.

STEP 2. Add compost, so the pot is about a third full.

STEP 3. Position the first layer of bulbs, with the roots at the bottom and narrow necks at the top, at approximately three times their depth or a little deeper as a second layer is going to be added.

STEP 4. Cover with the compost, just leaving the top of the bulbs visible.

STEP 5. Next, add the second layer of bulbs, making sure not to place them right on top of the bulbs that you've already planted.

STEP 6. Continue to add compost so that the pot is almost full and the bulbs are completely covered.

STEP 7. Water in bulbs, and start longing for spring!

✶ HARVESTING 🍓

The next phase of harvesting involves gathering the first crops of your autumn vegetables. Late summer crops can also provide fruit and vegetables for early autumn harvests, such as lettuces, raspberries and beans, depending on when you sowed them and how warm a summer we've had.

Harvests are never going to be as abundant as during the middle of summer, but it's great to be able to nip out on a chilly night and return with your own fresh produce from the garden.

Lettuces may give up the ghost and growth on mustard leaves may slow down, but hardy crops such as leeks, chard, kale and Jerusalem artichokes are great vegetables for supplying warming feasts throughout the coldest months and into spring. There'll also be some herbs to harvest, adding delicious flavours to your autumn and winter cooking.

Jerusalem artichokes

These delicious knobbly vegetables are nuggets of pure joy. Just digging them up is so exciting. My sister Esther describes their taste as somewhere between a pear and a potato and I don't think I can better that. After the first frosts, the tall stems should be cut right down and, unlike potatoes, these tubers can be left in the ground until ready to eat from now until March'. Nowhere to be seen in supermarkets until November and very pricey when they do appear, this vegetable is definitely worth growing. You may get a bigger crop if you sow them in the ground, but they will also do very well grown in a large growbag or container. Just remember they can grow to 6-8 feet (180-240cm) tall. Once harvested, pop two or three tubers back into the bag or soil for more Jerusalem artichokes from next October onwards.

Rocket

These lovely peppery leaves enliven any salad or are great on their own with a dressing and a few shavings of Parmesan cheese. Once you've grown rocket, either the wild (thinner leaves and yellow flowers) or cultivated form (fuller leaves and cream-coloured flowers), you'll find seedlings popping up unexpectedly throughout the year.

Leeks

Leeks should be nice and chunky by now and ready for the first harvest of the season. And it's such a tasty crop – one that, home-grown, is far superior to shop-bought varieties. When digging up leeks, use a fork to loosen the soil and help the vegetables out of the ground by pulling them from the base. If you pull from the top of the leek, they may snap. I've found 'Musselburgh', an old heritage variety, to be a really reliable grower, producing lovely chunky stalks every year.

If you've noticed your once healthy crop fading away, read on, as it may be a leek moth infestation. Up until recently, leeks have been fairly pest-free, but over the last few years (since 2003 on the south coast and moving northwards), leek moth has raised its ugly head, laying eggs in your leeks, which grow into maggots that reduce crops to tatters. (They also affect onions and shallots.) The only way to be certain of avoiding this pest is to cover the whole crop with fleece from the word go. And commiserations if your crop has been affected.

Kale

Keep picking kale leaves from the outside of your plant and it will carry on producing smaller leaves, growing higher and higher. Great for winter greens that can be stir-fried. I like to add leaves to my shepherd's pie to give it extra green goodness. There are many types of kale, ranging from deepest green to a rich purple, some with flat leaves and others that are wonderfully frilly. This is certainly a plant that is worth planting for its stunning decorative qualities alone but it also has a great earthy taste. Plant seeds in early spring for smaller summer leaves (great for both salads and stir-fries) or sow in summer for overwintering.

Swiss chard

Swiss chard is a sight for sore eyes as many other vegetables and flowers shut up shop for the winter. The colourful stems light up the whole garden on a crisp sunny day. Worth growing for its handsome stature, but also a jolly useful hardy leaf to enjoy through the winter and even well into spring. The smaller delicate leaves will brighten up a salad and the larger leaves can be used like spinach. The tougher stems can be removed before cooking the leaves and cooked on their own: chop them up, fry in butter and serve with a topping of parmesan cheese for a warm winter treat.

Salad burnet

This hardy evergreen herb has beautifully decorative serrated blue-grey leaves. Its taste reminds you of mild cucumber with a slightly metallic aftertaste. Queen of herbs, Jekka McVicar, advises growing this plant in semi-shade as the leaves will become bitter in the glare of the hot summer. It can do well long into autumm.

Winter lettuces & mustard leaves

During colder months, it's wonderful to have slender pickings of fresh leaves from your front garden. Lettuces may have difficulty surviving hard frosts, but mustard leaves will tough it out through most autumn and winter weathers, adding tangy tastes to salads. There are so many varieties of mustard leaf available now, such as 'Red Giant', 'Flaming Frills', 'Golden Streak', 'Green in Snow', 'Mizuna' and 'Mibuna', that you're spoilt for choice. Sow seeds in August and September to brighten up chilly winter days.

Sage

A hardy evergreen herb that can be eaten all year round, it has lovely purple-blue flowers in summer and is adored by bees. It's great for flavouring comforting winter stews and makes a tea that will calm upset stomachs. Sage (*Salvia officinalis*) comes in many colours and sizes. I love growing purple sage alongside the green variety for a gentle undulating contrast. Sage grows well in pots, but doesn't like peat, so use a soil-based compost, such as John Innes, when planting. Look at www.herbalhaven.com for some other exciting varieties to plant come spring.

Parsley

You should still be getting plenty of this biennial herb (ie one that goes to seed in its second year). Note that flat-leafed parsley is frost-hardy and slightly tougher than its curly-leafed cousin.

Rosemary

A very hardy herb and one that is of great use in the kitchen. It's an evergreen plant, so it can add year-round structure to your garden and has tiny delicate pale blue flowers in spring and summer.

Above: Vincci cutting herbs in her front garden
Right: Parsley in a suitcase

THIS MONTH'S LIST

NOVEMBER

Things have really quietened down in the garden and it's a great time for looking back. What were the most successful crops in your garden or on your window sills; what different or additional crops would you like to try out next year? If you think you'd like more fruit, then now is the best time to order canes and bushes such as raspberries, Japanese wineberries, blueberries and blackberries. Why? Because the growing season has slowed down, which means that plants are dormant and can easily be dug up and delivered with just their bare roots, i.e not in pots or soil. This reduces delivery costs and makes them cheaper – and more environmentally friendly as no plastic pots are required. There's often a greater choice of varieties too. They'll need to be planted within a few days of their arrival, though, or planted on into pots if the soil is frozen.

At both Chelsea and Hampton Court flower shows I've seen ingenious ways of training these sometimes unruly fruit canes to fit into small spaces. You can have great fun twisting blackberries, for example, into figures of eight that can be planted neatly by the front door to form a horticultural sculpture. It sounds complicated, but it's not. You'll just need a few bamboo canes and string to create your shapes. Cut the stems back to the ground after they've fruited – and start again the following season!

🏠 COMMUNITY CORNER 🛞

While all else is quiet in the garden, it's a great time for a big clear-up. If you want to get outside on a bright sunny day, leaves can be collected and packed into black bags to create leafmould. This is a very easy way to make your own (free) fabulous compost, but it does require a fair amount of patience. Fill the bags with wet leaves (or add water to the bag if the leaves are dry), puncture the bag with a fork to create plenty of holes for aeration and then just wait! (It's best not to rake up evergreen leaves, though, as this tougher foliage will take much longer to break down). Over time – about a year for using as a mulch and two years to create a finer potting compost – leaves will take on a gorgeous crumbly texture.

As the end of the year approaches, canvass neighbours as you bump into them about what worked best for them in growbags and window boxes and ask if there's anything different that they'd like to try next year. Annie found that while she was manning the plant advice stall at the Chelsea Fringe Cake Sunday, people were very impressed by the carrots in window boxes and Nicolette loved the idea of Japanese wineberries compactly trained to fit into our tight urban spaces. I've found that tumbling tomato 'Terenzo' produced a fantastic amount of tasty fruit growing in window boxes and we'll be adding these to our seed order for next spring, as well as buying small tomato plants to plant directly outside in May. Colin (and many other neighbours) were charmed by the 'Red Mini Turban' squashes, and we have our fingers crossed for a warmer summer next year as we plan on experimenting with a few different varieties come spring. Eleni was wowed by the spectacular growth of our 'Tromboncino' courgettes, and has plans to grow more of these next year, and Sue, having gazed longingly at luscious raspberries this year, now has her own canes in pots to supply fruits for her and her family next summer. (See planting raspberries in pots page 200.)

*Top right: David tying in a Japanese
wineberry to form a figure of eight
Bottom right: Kids collecting autumn leaves*

I love raspberries. I've found autumn raspberries (as opposed to summer-fruiting raspberries) are the best fruit canes to grow when space is limited as they're fairly compact (if kept in check!) and don't need to be supported by wires. This also means that they can grow happily in mixed borders with flowers and other veg and still give you an amazing amount of fruit per plant, even cropping well in their first year of growth.

Autumn-fruiting varieties

'Autumn Bliss' is a long-established autumn raspberry favourite, but the new kids on the block include 'Joan J' and 'Polka'. 'Polka' has very large pointed berries, almost twice the size of my 'Autumn Bliss', and is a very tasty new variety. Some people swear by 'Polka', others resolutely stand by 'Autumn Bliss'. I like both of them: grow some of each and decide for yourself. Canes can be ordered from www.pomonafruits.co.uk, www.blackmoor.co.uk or www.victoriananursery.co.uk, normally in packs of 5 or 6, or bought at Potato Days (see page 22). If you want to try out different varieties, but don't need 10 or 12 canes, then why not get together with neighbours and share an order?

Planting into the soil

Raspberries do best in full sun, but will still happily fruit away as long as they have at least three hours of sun a day and rich but free draining soil.

With all bare-rooted plants, soak the roots for 20-30 minutes before planting. You can plant any time from November through until March, but never plant if the ground is frozen or waterlogged, as the plants won't survive.

If possible, prepare the soil with plenty of compost or well-rotted manure mixed in a few weeks before you plant your canes. Raspberries are not deep-rooted. They have roots that spread mainly horizontally only a few inches below the surface of the soil (which makes them very adept at spreading all over the place!). Plant canes to the same depth they were planted before (you should see the mark the soil has left behind on the canes), placing them about 18 inches (45cm) apart. If you have space to plant more than one row, plant each row about 5-6ft (150-180cm) apart. After planting your canes, cut them down to a few inches above the ground and prune this way every February (see page 39). See page 200 for how to plant raspberries in pots.

Ordering other bare-rooted fruit

This month is a great time to order and plant other bare-rooted fruits, such as Japanese wineberries. Unlike autumn-fruiting raspberries, these canes will take a couple of years to get fruiting, but will be a great addition to your fruit and veg patch, giving you more fruit over summer. They can be trained on wires up a wall or as a figure of eight using bamboo canes, allowing them to snugly fit into any front garden. Their pruning regime is different from that of autumn raspberries. You have to cut back the older stems that have fruited late in summer (see page 153) and keep the new stems which will fruit the following year.

Top: Autumn raspberries growing in a pot
Bottom: Bare-rooted raspberries canes for sale

SIMPLE BUT BRILLIANT IDEAS

||||||||||||||||||||||||||||||||||||||||||||||||||||||||||||||||||||||||||||||||

Tim's topiary elephants

Tim started transforming a neighbour's troublesome and massively overgrown hedge in January, and by July, a herd of elephants had appeared. Tim makes his art of topiary look incredibly simple (and wields his hedge trimmer with genuine skill), but by changing an unsightly and enormous hedge into a piece of sculpture, he has enriched the whole neighbourhood. Simple but brilliant.

More of Tim's work can be seen at www.outofmyshed. co.uk/2011/08/10/tims-topiary-or-bushes-bushes/ and Tim can be contacted at tim@walkerbushe.co.uk

ONE POT SHOP

GARLIC

Roasted fresh garlic is reason alone for growing this tasty and very useful veg. Plant bulbs from November until the end of March.

You will need:

1. Garlic bulbs. 'Solent Wight' (available from www.thegarlicfarm.co.uk) grows well in the UK and has a great flavour

2. Crock for drainage

3. Compost: John Innes no.3, garden or recycled compost from the council

4. A pot at least 6 inches wide and deep. The bigger the pot, the more bulbs you can grow, planting bulbs 3-4 inches (7-10cm) apart. You can plant three bulbs in a 6-inch (15cm) pot, six in an 8-inch (20cm) pot and nine in a 10-inch (25cm) pot

5. A sunny position. Garlic needs full sun to grow well

STEP 1. Put some crock in the bottom of your pot for drainage.

STEP 2. Fill your pot with compost, leaving an inch free at the top to allow for watering.

STEP 3. Carefully break up your garlic bulb into cloves just before you plant them, trying not to damage any, as this could encourage rotting.

STEP 4. Space cloves out evenly and plant, roots down and pointy end up, about an inch and a half (3-4cm) deep, just below the surface of the compost. Fill in the hole you've created with compost.

STEP 5. Keep well watered. If your pot is on a window sill (or covered balcony), check it regularly as it may be in a rain shadow and need more watering than you think.

STEP 6. Feed pots in February with sulphate of potash (available at all good garden centres) to encourage big fat juicy bulbs.

Bulbs should be ready to harvest about mid-July, when you see the stems flop over. Keep watering up until a few weeks before harvesting and then stop watering completely. If you see flowers forming, snip them off, as you want the plant to put all its energy into bulb, not flower, production.

THIS MONTH'S LIST

DECEMBER

Some years, it can be warmer at Christmas than during the spring, and despite the shorter days, self-seeded rocket and sweet peas will miraculously start popping up in the front garden. Other years, all will be covered in a blanket of snow with hardly a sign of life. Generally, though, it's a quiet time in the garden for growing.

Once I've worked the last gardening days of the year, having some spare time affords me the leisure to think about the approaching new year. Spring may seem like a long way off, but in February I often sow sweet peas indoors as well as lettuces in my mini greenhouse, so now is the time to send off for catalogues as well as peruse online sites (see page 21 for interesting seed companies).

While you're tucked up inside, think about the wildlife in your garden. Hang up feeders for birds and regularly top them up with seeds, and use any container, be it an old shallow bowl or a plastic plant saucer, as a bird bath, making sure you break the ice during cold spells. You'll be rewarded with frequent visits to your garden by these feathered beauties, who, furthermore, will be feeding on slugs, aphids and other pests in your garden come spring.

COMMUNITY CORNER

December is a relaxed gardening month, when you can put your feet up and start dreaming of the perfect, utopian veg plot. However, if you fancy a gentle gardening task, December is the perfect month for mulching (see page 204). There's no need for any heavy digging or overexertion. Simply add a good layer, 2-3 inches (5-8cm) of compost or manure to the top of the soil in your tree pits (and borders) and the worms will do the rest of the work for you. They'll break down this organic matter into a rich food source for your plants. The thick mulch will also help to keep weeds at bay, allowing you a lovely blank canvas on which to start sowing your wildflower seeds in spring.

While many of our tree pits are grown as mini wildflower meadows, others are packed full with perennial flowers. These can take a little while to get established, but think about plants that will survive in this fairly harsh environment and have fun in designing a pocket-sized garden to enliven your street. Mediterranean, drought-tolerant plants, such as lavender and the gorgeous daisy, erigeron, seem to thrive, and hollyhocks have also been a great success in our tree pits, adding height and beautiful blooms.

Still have a little energy? Then it's worthwhile cleaning all your empty pots so that any pests and diseases aren't carried through to next year's growing season. Time spent now will enable you to spring into action next year as the weather warms up. So tip any dead plants and old soil into your compost or recycling bins. If any plants look diseased it's best not add them to your compost. Give both plastic and ceramic pots a good wash, checking the bases as you go for pests and their eggs. I just use washing-up liquid but some people add 10 per cent bleach to the washing-up bowl or use stronger disinfectants such as Jeyes Fluid. Mini greenhouses could also benefit from a good wash, to clean away pests and diseases, and also allow maximum light for your plants to grow early next year.

For a rainy-day project, have a look at the mini greenhouse that Colin and I built using recycled plastic bottles on page 194.

Top: Liesbet mulching a tree pit
Bottom: Annie washing pots
Previous page: 'Red Giant Mustard Leaf'
toughing it out in the snow

🏠 RAINY-DAY PROJECT 🌱

HOW TO BUILD A MINI GREENHOUSE
OUT OF PLASTIC BOTTLES

While all else is quiet in the garden, it's a great time to get on with some rainy-day projects. Inspired by the large plastic bottle greenhouse at 'Food from the Sky' (see February, page 42) neighbour Colin and I thought we'd have a go at building a mini greenhouse that would be just large enough for a couple of seed trays. Our friendly local café, Cinnamon Village, very kindly saved small used water bottles for us over a couple of months and we got together one afternoon to have a go at constructing the greenhouse. As we wanted to keep it simple and cheap, we used just bamboo canes, the recycled bottles and some nylon twine.

You'll need to prepare the bottles first, so put aside a few hours to remove the labels. Then put aside about four hours (if there are two people) for building the structure. We used nylon twine to bind the canes as it doesn't stretch, but it can be quite hard on your skin,

so you may need a pair of gloves (gardening or washing-up).

We were really pleased with our first attempt at a mini greenhouse. It's not entirely enclosed as there are gaps where the bottles meet (especially on top), but this isn't a bad thing, as it will allow rain to come in and a bit of ventilation, while still protecting seedlings and small plants from the worst of the weather. You could always use bubble wrap or any transparent plastic sheeting for the top if you wanted a more enclosed structure, but we loved the aesthetic of the bottles and the economy of recycling. Luckily, plastic bottles are very flexible and you can push them into each other to create columns of different lengths, depending on how tall you want to go. It's great to have a protected environment to start seeds off in early spring, so if you have a bit of space and some spare time, why not give it a go?

We used:

176 half-litre water bottles

Washing-up liquid

A sharp kitchen knife

A chopping board

7x 8ft (240cm) bamboo canes

A pair of secateurs to cut the bamboo canes

Nylon string

A pair of scissors

Gloves (for tying the nylon twine, as it can be tough on your hands)

STEP 1. Prepare the bottles beforehand as this will take a couple of sessions of a good few hours. Carefully cut off the bottom end of the bottles with a kitchen knife on a chopping board and remove the cap. Tear off as much paper as you can manage, and then soak the bottles in hot soapy water (I used washing-up liquid) for an hour or so to help remove the remaining paper and as much glue as possible. (I couldn't remove all the glue, but just take off as much as you can to reduce light loss in the greenhouse.)

STEP 2. We made a start on building a framework out of bamboo canes, making sure the base was big enough for two standard seed trays to comfortably fit in, and allowing 2 inches (5cm) all around the trays.

We cut the bamboo into the following lengths for our greenhouse, using the thickest pieces for the bottom:

For the bottom:
5 x 28 inches (71cm) widths
2 x 24 inches (61cm) for depth

For the top:
2 x 28 inches (71cm) widths
3 x 24 inches (61cm) depths

For the side:
4 x 27 inches (69cm) heights

STEP 3. We carefully tied joints together with nylon string (wearing gloves!), making sure that everything was held tightly together. For the bottom we tied the five width canes on top of the two depth canes. For the top we tied the width canes on top of the two outside depth canes and the central depth cane on top of the width canes, to create a small slope when the bottles were tied in.

STEP 4. When we had constructed both the bottom and top frameworks, we tied in the height canes, just inside the corner joins of the top and bottom frameworks.

STEP 5. Creating the bottle columns. We used four bottles to create the height of the bottle columns, firmly pushing and jamming the bottles, nose first, into one another for the first three bottles and then bottom end to bottom end for the last bottle. This meant that we had a 'nose' at both the top and bottom of our columns which held them fairly firmly.

STEP 6. Attaching the bottle columns. For the back and sides of the greenhouse, we tied some twine onto the top of the framework, threaded it through the column of bottles with the help of a spare piece of bamboo cane and then tightly tied the twine onto the bottom cane.

STEP 7. For the front, we tied in two columns at each side, then created a door by tying in the top of six columns as above, but then tying in the bottom of the twine to a separate piece of bamboo which could easily be lifted up to access the inside of the greenhouse.

STEP 8. To help the columns keep their shape, we wove the twine around the bottles at the middle of each column on the back and sides of the greenhouse, tying it into the bamboo height poles at both ends. For the door we wove the twine around the columns at two points for extra strength.

SIMPLE BUT BRILLIANT IDEAS

||||||||||||||||||||||||||||||||||||||||||||||||||||||||||||||||||||||||||||

Crockery plant labels by Esther Coombs

Why not have a go at making your own? Firstly, dig out some old chipped or broken crockery (or pop out to a charity shop and pick up some old plates), and break them into large chunks. I wrapped a saucer in a tea towel and tapped gently-ish with a hammer to break it. Permanent marker pens (in different thicknesses) can be bought for a couple of pounds from your local stationer's. Have a go at writing and drawing your own customised labels for the plants that you like to grow. I cut up some bamboo canes into 9-inch (23cm) lengths for my labels and used Araldite glue (any other epoxy resin adhesive will do) to attach the crockery to them. However, you could use any spare lengths of wood you can lay your hands on, instead of bamboo. Make sure you rub down both the crockery and bamboo with coarse sandpaper before you join them together so that the glue can really take hold, otherwise they'll come apart after a heavy frost. And try and glue together the largest areas possible, for extra strength. You'll be delighted with your results. A great small project for a quiet afternoon.

ONE POT SHOP

AUTUMN-FRUITING RASPBERRIES IN A BOX

Autumn-fruiting (as opposed to summer-fruiting) raspberries are ideal for pots as they don't need any supports and they'll fruit in the first year. Your pots don't have to be too deep (6 inches/15cm minimum, though) as raspberries have shallow roots, but their roots can spread fairly widely, so any container of about a foot square (30cm x 30cm) and bigger would be an ideal size.

You will need:

1. A bare-root raspberry cane for each container (see page 185 for suppliers)

2. A large container. The container could be a wooden wine box, a medium to large growbag, an old suitcase or plant directly into a bag of John Innes no.3 compost

3. Crock to line the bottom of the container for good drainage

4. Plenty of rich compost. Don't use multi-purpose compost as this just isn't rich enough for a plant that's going to stay in the same pot for a number of years

STEP 1. Make sure your container has drainage holes and put a couple of handfuls of crock at the bottom.

STEP 2. Fill the container to approximately three-quarters full with compost.

STEP 3. Plant one cane per container to the same depth they were planted before (you should see a mark the soil has left behind on the canes), covering the roots well, but leaving 2 inches (5cm) free of compost at the top of the container. This will allow you to mulch later in the year with more compost.

STEP 4. Water in well. And from April, when the plant starts to put on growth, feed every one to two weeks with liquid seaweed until the raspberries have finished fruiting. Cut back stems in February (see page 39) for a great crop the following year.

GARDEN JARGON EXPLAINED

SUCCESSIONAL SOWING

If you sow all your seeds at once, all
your crops will be ready to eat at about the same
time. However, if you sow a row or pot of a crop
and then wait a few weeks before sowing the
next lot, you should be able to space out
your harvesting period, too, thus avoiding gluts.
Once the growing season gets under way and
things become really hectic, I write a note to
myself in my diary as to when to sow the next
batch of seeds.

SOWING THINLY

'Sow thinly' means spacing out your
seeds evenly when you sow them, so that they
are not too closely bunched together.
Pour some of the seeds onto the palm of your
hand and use your fingers to carefully position
the seeds on the compost so that a whole bunch
of seeds doesn't land on one small area all at
once. Your seeds will go a lot further if you sow
this way, and you'll have less thinning out to do.

THINNING OUT

Even if you've sow your seeds thinly (see
above), there'll probably be too many seedlings
growing near to each other, competing for water
and nutrients. You can either prick out (see
below) or thin out. To thin out, look for the most
healthy-looking seedling, and then pull out all
the other seedlings around it, trying not
to disturb roots of the seedling that is left. These
excess seedlings need not be wasted and can be
added as tasty 'micro greens' to your salad bowl.

PRICKING OUT

Ideally, you want your seedlings to have enough space to be able to grow bigger without competition for water, nutrients and light from other plants. Prick out seedlings into either individual pots or modules.

First, using a pencil or pen, make a hole in the compost. Carefully twirl the delicate seedling roots into the hole, holding it by the leaves only. If you have long leggy seedlings, try to bury as much of the stem as possible, as it will grow into roots once below the soil. This will give you a stronger plant in the long run. Never handle seedlings by the roots, though, as they are delicate and may break. Using your thumbs and index fingers, press down on the compost on either side of the seedlings to make it firm. Water them and keep them well watered as they grow. Seedlings will be ready to plant out when you see roots just peeking out at the bottom of the pot or module.

POTTING ON

Potting on is done when seedlings in modules or small pots are ready to be planted out in the ground or in a larger pot.

STEP 1. Dig a hole large enough to accommodate your seedling.

STEP 2. Place your fingers on either side of the seedling before turning the pot upside down.

STEP 3. Still holding the seedling in place with your fingers, tip the pot upside down to empty it out.

STEP 4. Carefully place the seedling in the hole, trying not to disturb the roots.

STEP 5. Fill in the hole around the seedling with compost and firm it down with your fingers so that the roots make contact with soil.

STEP 6. Water in well.

HARDENING OFF

Hardening off means acclimatising plants that you have started off indoors to outdoor temperatures and the wind. First, over a period of about 7 to 10 days, move your seedlings outside during the day and bring them in at night to help them adjust to their new environment. Only then should you plant them out outside. It's best not to put a tiny seedling in the hot sun in its first few outings, as the scorching rays will cause it to dry out too quickly and shrivel up.

MULCHING

Mulching is adding a layer of compost or well-rotted manure – of about 2-3 inches (5-7.5cm) – around the base of a plant, usually in early spring or autumn. This helps conserve moisture in the soil and acts as a slow-release fertiliser as worms slowly break down the compost, turning it into nutrients that plant roots can then access.

Life cycles

ANNUALS

Annual plants are sown from seed (usually in spring, but sometimes in autumn) and grow, flower, set seed and die all within one year. They don't come back the following year, but they may self-seed and start their life cycle all over again the following spring. *For example*: poppies, cornflowers, lettuces, sweet peas, mustard leaf and rocket.

PERENNIALS

Perennials are plants that will come back year after year. You can grow perennials from seed, but it's often quicker and easier to buy them as small plants, to grow from cuttings and offshoots or by dividing bigger plants. *For example*: rhubarb (divide), strawberries (offshoots called runners), lavender and rosemary (cuttings).

BIENNIALS

Biennials are plants that have a two-year life cycle, where they produce leafy growth in the first year and then flower, set seed and die in their second year. *For example*: parsley, foxgloves, angelica, carrots (which would flower in the second year if they weren't dug up), evening primrose and teasels.

VEG BLOGS

I love writing my own gardening blog (www.outofmyshed.co.uk), and I enjoy reading many others. Some are very practical, others witty, but all are very seasonal. Here's a list of some of my favourites:

www.realmensow.co.uk – a cheery and entertaining allotment blog

www.verticalveg.org.uk – packed full of great how-to's for tight spaces

www.mytinyplot.com – timely posts from a small veg garden, plus a great 'create your own blog' tutorial

www.vegplotting.blogspot.co.uk – lots on veg growing, especially salads

www.gardengrab.co.uk – a hub for many great gardening blogs

www.throughthegardengate.co.uk/blog – insightful views on London gardens

www.oxoniangardener.co.uk – more in-depth posts on all things horticultural

www.wellywoman.wordpress.com – thoughful views on all things gardening

VEG BOOKS

Some of my essential bedtime reads are listed below:

Grow Your Own Vegetables by **Joy Larkcom** – my veg-growing bible, packed full of useful growing information. She's simply the best

Veg Patch by **Mark Diacono** – a great A-Z of veg to grow with fab pics

A Taste of the Unexpected by **Mark Diacono** – how to make your garden full of difficult-to-buy fruit and veg

The Edible Garden by **Alys Fowler** – how to happily mix veg and flowers – great lists

Salad Leaves for All Seasons by **Charles Dowding** – inspirational and informative for all aspiring salad growers

Urban Eden by **Adam and James Caplin** – tempting images for growing in urban spaces

The Rurbanite by **Alex Mitchell** – how to live in the country without leaving the city

Homegrown Revolution by **James Wong** – Loads of new and exciting fruit and veg to try.

HOW TO FORM A CONSTITUTED GROUP

It's easy to form a constituted group. You'll just need four neighbours to form a committee and agree on who will be chair, vice-chair, secretary and treasurer. Ask other neighbours if they would like to become committee members and encourage them to come along to meetings.

Together, you'll need to draw up a constitution with a list of your aims. I've found that www.upstream-uk.com/A-simple-Constitution.html has a good starting blueprint.

You'll need to meet a few times a year, but meetings don't have to be lengthy. Just type up an agenda, and get together over a cup of tea in someone's kitchen to discuss future events, fundraising and any other matters. The treasurer will need to keep basic accounts showing receipts for all you've spent from your funding at the end of each year and the secretary should record in writing the decisions made at the meetings. It's as simple as that.

We've found that the Co-operative Bank (www.co-operativebank.co.uk) offers a good bank account for community groups with a constitution, and that Towergate Insurance (www.towergaterisksolutions.co.uk) offers reasonably priced public liability insurance for community groups in the UK (most funders will request that community groups have public liability insurance).

INDEX

ACKNOWLEDGEMENTS

Huge thanks to all my neighbours, especially Annie, Bernd, David, Helen, Kate, Kimmy, Liesbet, Julia, Manuel, Nicolette, Paul and Robert, without whom I couldn't have written this book. And a whole heap of gratitude to my parents who got me hooked on vegetable growing from an early age. Very warm thanks to Adrian and Rozelle for taking my pics at the drop of a hat and much appreciation to Julia, Lizzie, Lucy, Sarah, Simon, Valerie and Veronica for all their help and encouragement. Many thanks to my IT guru, Kevin, for his generosity of spirit and his time. And finally, massive thanks and love to Des for putting up with me while writing this book.

Published in 2013 by
Short Books
3A Exmouth House
Pine Street
EC1R 0JH

10 9 8 7 6 5 4 3 2 1

Copyright ©
Naomi Schillinger 2013

Design: Georgia Vaux

Naomi Schillinger has asserted her right under the Copyright, Designs and Patents Act 1988 to be identified as the author of this work. All rights reserved. No part of this publication may be reproduced, stored in a retrieval system or transmitted in any form, or by any means (electronic, mechanical, or otherwise) without the prior written permission of both the copyright owners and the publisher.

A CIP catalogue record for this book is available from the British Library.

ISBN 978-1-78072-112-5

Printed in Great Britain by Butler, Tanner & Dennis Ltd

Photo Credits
All images are taken by the author, Naomi Schillinger, except: Adrian Pope, www.adrianpope.co.uk: pages: 4, 5, 6, 52 (bottom right), 135 (bottom left), 143, 157 (top photos), 184 (top photo), back cover top left. Roger Phillips: page: 9 (bottom right). Sarah Cuttle, www.sarahcuttle.co.uk: page: 87 (top photo). Pat Tuson, www.pattuson.co.uk: page 104